Additional Praise for *Between Panic and Desire*

"The writing is frequently very funny; insightful, too, especially Moore's belief that humans are generally delusional when it comes to their expectations vs. what is realistically possible. . . . The narrative has its poignant moments, particularly in Moore's recollections of his father. And despite his fractured take on the world, his message is essentially hopeful. Moore, it seems, is moving on."—Robert Kelly, *Library Journal*

"*Between Panic and Desire* is more autopsy than memoir—a strange new hybrid. It's a fantasy of letting go of the things that have haunted Moore his entire life. These things do, in fact, float off the pages."—*Los Angeles Times*

"[Moore] is a master of pastiche memoir. . . . Moore cooks up the ingredients of his derelict youth and (allegedly) reformed maturity with an edgy sense of humor that keeps his memories and observations from slipping into sentimentality or anger. He knows how to meta up a story without making it too self-conscious, how to mix and match the political, personal and pop cultural without descending into trite."—Barbara Goodman Shovers, *Mid-American Review*

"This book is funny, funny, funny. It is an unconventional—some might say, experimental—collection of frolicsome and touching personal essays. . . . The book is a rare example of how unusual form actually helps. It is the ideal display for Dinty's imagination. He daydreams. He fantasizes. He hallucinates. And this is nonfiction. For anyone who thinks the genre is nothing more than a retelling of facts, pick up a copy of *Between Panic and Desire*. . . . It is literary nonfiction with integrity. And it's fun."—*Oxford Town*

"The gem of the book might be 'Double Vision.' This chapter about the author's diplopia (double vision) lets readers sink into a more familiar personal essay format. Here, Moore mixes wry, almost self-deprecating humor and carefully wrought descriptions of himself as a young man to infuse the piece with touching humanity."—Robin Mozer, *Black Warrior Review*

"In intertwined, wildly inventive essays ... Moore conjures up his, and our, past from a grab-bag of elements. ... He doesn't work through this crazy salad so much as play with it, using individual motifs as shiny mosaic stones to arrange in funny, intriguing shapes." —*Athens News*

"The book's finest chapter, 'Number Nine,' is a disturbing, yet unexpectedly funny meditation on Yoko Ono, Charles Manson and Sept. 11. Moore's control of his narrative voice is exceptional. He tells a moving, sometimes downright sad story without veering into nostalgia, sentimentality or too-clever archness." —Rebecca Oppenheimer, *Howard County (MD) Times*

"Hear that? That is the sweet sonic boom of the Baby Boom barrier being broken by this elegant flight of essays launched from the steely hand of Captain Dinty W. Moore in his remarkable memoir *Between Panic and Desire*. Impossible, they said, to reveal this precisely that sense of time, place, and even space. Listen: Read, read, read. Words away! That's it. Exactly. Like that." —Michael Martone, author of *Michael Martone: Fictions*

"Dinty W. Moore's prose is crisp and clean, his insights sparkle with biting clarity and magnetic charm. This is an unusual, joyful, and compelling memoir." —Lee Gutkind, author of *Almost Human: Making Robots Think* and editor of *Creative Nonfiction Magazine*

"This is a refreshing and invigorating book, taking the predictable memoir form in new directions—playfully, sincerely, and intelligently. This is a terrific book." —Bret Lott, author of *Jewel*

AMERICAN LIVES | TOBIAS WOLFF, SERIES EDITOR

University of Nebraska Press | Lincoln and London

To ROGER—
Nice to meet you
in Cedarville.

BETWEEN
PANIC
AND
DESIRE

Dinty W. Moore

Dinty
2012

Photograph of John Hinckley Jr. on page 63
used with the permission of AP Images.

Acknowledgments for previously published
material appear on page xii, which constitutes
an extension of the copyright page.

Library of Congress Cataloging-in-Publication Data
Moore, Dinty W., 1955–
Between panic and desire / Dinty W. Moore.
    p. cm. — (American lives)
Includes index.
ISBN 978-0-8032-1149-0 (cloth : alk. paper)
ISBN 978-0-8032-2982-2 (paper : alk. paper)
1. United States—Social conditions—1960–1980.
2. United States—Social conditions—1980–
3. United States—Civilization—1945—
Miscellanea. 4. Popular culture—United States—
History—20th century. 5. Moore, Dinty W., 1955–
I. Title.
E169.12.M65 2007
973.92—dc22   2007023288

Set in Univers and Minion.
Designed by A. Shahan.

For Buddy, until next time

History would be so much simpler if
you could just write it
Without ever having to let it happen.

Kenneth Rexroth

"Another Early Morning Exercise"

CONTENTS

ACKNOWLEDGMENTS

First, to Renita, with constant love and gratitude, and Maria, with respect and admiration.

Sincere thanks as well to friends and colleagues who offered encouragement and expertise: Ken Womack, Todd Davis, Laurie Drummond, Kate Latterell, Antonio Vallone, Steve Sherrill, Diana Hume George, Dawn Marano, and Judith Kitchen. My gratitude to Penn State Altoona and Chancellor Lori Bechtel for support of my creative activity.

Natalia Rachel Singer's early review of this manuscript was crucial. Ladette Randolph provided ongoing and deeply appreciated support and encouragement. Carol Mann stood by as well, when panic began to overtake desire. And Lee Gutkind has been there all along.

And finally, thank you, thank you (and thank you) to the magazine editors who gave of their limited time and unlimited intelligence to help shape portions of this freewheeling narrative: Bret Lott, Joe Mackall, Peter Stitt, Avery Rome, and Kristen Iversen. But especially Marty Lammon, a deeply generous man.

Chapters from this book, often in significantly different form, have previously appeared in the following publications:

"Prologue: Between Panic and Desire" first appeared as "A Fork in the Mood: Before I Came to Panic, I Reached Desire" in *Philadelphia Inquirer Magazine*, June 4, 1995, 4.

"Son of Mr. Green Jeans: A Meditation on Missing Fathers" first appeared as "Son of Mr. Green Jeans: An Essay on Fatherhood, Alphabetically Arranged" in *Crazyhorse*, no. 63 (Spring 2003): 49–53.

"Son of Richard M. Nixon" first appeared as "Nixon's the One" in *Gettysburg Review* 20, no. 3 (Autumn 2007).

"Three Bad Trips, 1968–77" first appeared in *River Teeth: A Journal of Nonfiction Narrative* 8, no. 2 (Spring 2007). © 2007 by the University of Nebraska Press. Reprinted by permission.

"Baseball, Hot Dogs, Mescaline, and Chevrolet" first appeared as "Baseball, Hot Dogs, Mescaline, and Chevrolet: An Essay Utilizing a Passage from Aldous Huxley's *Doors of Perception* as Section Headings" in *Arts & Letters: Journal of Contemporary Culture*, no. 9 (Spring 2003): 86–96.

"Number Nine" first appeared in *Pinch* 27, no. 2 (Fall 2007).

"Son of George McManus" first appeared as "Mick on the Make" in *Southern Review* 43, no. 3 (Summer 2007).

"Three Days in September" first appeared as "The White House: Three Days in September, 2001" in *Arts & Letters: Journal of Contemporary Culture*, no. 7 (Spring 2002): 131–42.

"'Curtis Knows Best': Towering, Permanent, Perilous, and Soon to be Televised on a Widescreen Near You" first appeared as "'Curtis Knows Best': A Television Docu-Drama Exploring the Towering and Permanent Dangers of Middle Mind" in *Arts & Letters: Journal of Contemporary Culture*, no. 8 (Fall 2002): 46–62.

Deep in the scrub hills of Jefferson County, about eight miles north of Punxsutawney, lay two towns, Panic and Desire, separated by farms, trees, and a narrow road.

Returning from Pittsburgh one morning, I tug my steering wheel to the left, swing off the main highway, and motor up a steep rise. I have seen Panic and Desire on a map, and for some reason I want to visit.

Desire comes first, and proves to be little more than a few old houses and a modest cemetery. I'm curious how the town got such a name, what it is like to live here, what the people know that I don't, so I roll my compact car down the main road, looking for someone to ask.

But no one is out.

The graveyard appears to be my only alternative. I search the ancient stones for clues until a large white dog appears from nowhere. He shows me his teeth, follows me to my car, and barks his sharp warning until I leave.

So I head to Panic, a five-minute drive past tumbledown homes and modest trailers—families who have lost their farms, and those who are barely hanging on.

Like Desire, Panic turns out to be just a few ragtag family houses along a strip of asphalt. One of the homes has been completely gutted by fire and blackened furniture litters the front lawn. It looks as if it has been this way for months.

A white-haired gentleman bundled into an orange hunting jacket ambles down the road, so I step out of my car, walk toward him. "Any idea," I ask, "why they call this place Panic?"

He gives me an odd look.

"How about Desire?" I ask.

The man in orange shakes his head, offers a sad shrug, hurries down the road before I can squeeze in another question.

I'm intrigued, though, and fairly stubborn. In nearby DuBois there is a library, and I am heading more or less in that direction.

Twenty minutes later I'm in the stacks, unearthing a handful of local history books. For the next two hours I settle in at a wide table and read about the first European settlers—German and Scotch-Irish farmers pushing west across Pennsylvania in the early 1800s. The hills were full of deer, wild turkeys, and wolves.

There is no mention of Panic or Desire. The best I can find is the story of a man named Daniel North who was repairing his axe one morning when he heard his hogs let loose an unearthly squeal. North went to see what the matter was and saw a massive bear throwing one of the hogs across a field. The man attacked the bear with his axe, but only grazed the animal, and so the bear turned on him—man and bear, face to muzzle.

North, according to legend, started kicking at the bear, though it was easily twice his size, and eventually chased it off his farm into the woods, where it was never seen again.

Mr. North, one of the history books revealed, "thought it miraculous that the bear did not hug him to death."

Miraculous indeed. The shaggy bear story, if it is even true, occurred in a part of Jefferson County very near to where Panic and Desire were eventually established, and the story could explain the root of either place name perhaps.

Or perhaps not.

I ask the librarian. She doesn't know either.

So I return to my car, but instead of continuing east toward home, I double back, revisiting the road that separates Panic from Desire.

At what I approximate to be the halfway point, I pull over, switch off the ignition, and get out one more time into the cold March air. I am in the middle of a small patch of hemlock, a secluded spot, and it is here that I finally realize I don't want the actual answer, the truth of where these towns found their names. The mystery is sweeter.

I just bask in the unknown for a while, alone on the road, halfway between Panic and Desire.

Until it occurs to me: I have been here all my life.

Between Panic and Desire

part one. **PANIC**

1

INTRODUCTION
Hello, My Name Is_____

Human beings, truth be told, are inept narrators of their own lives. We don't often see what is right in front of us; frequently what we think we've seen is not actually there. In almost every case we see a decidedly distorted view, as if peering out through a rippled window.

Freud based much of his work on the idea that we instinctively project our own thoughts and feelings into the minds of others. Too often we end up hating those other people for what we presume they believe.

Buddhist philosophy revolves around a similar concept: we humans are guided by delusion—the delusion of "self"—yet we tenaciously insist that this is not the case.

The monk Thich Nhat Hanh, exiled from his native Vietnam in the early 1960s for advocating nonviolent civil disobedience, puts it simply and best:

"With a fearful panicking mind," he warns, "we can easily mistake a rope for a snake."

Well that's me, all over.

I see the world through undeniably distorted lenses, the particular curves and hollows of my distortions fashioned by forces personal and political, intimate and widespread. My mental optics are warped by the fear and panic induced by the Kennedy assassinations, the King assassination, Kent State, the rise and fall of Richard M. Nixon, *Father Knows Best* and *Leave It to Beaver*, Chuck Manson, the breakup of the Beatles, and the drinking, depression, and divorces that shaped my early family life. Add in countless nights of smoking too much dope and driving pointlessly in circles, and you've mapped the roots of my delusion fairly well.

But here's the rub: for the most part this list of formative events is communal. An entire generation lived through the untimely death of JFK (lost a good father), the resignation of Tricky Dick (lost a dysfunctional dad), and the turmoil of Vietnam (lost our Uncle Sam). We've all spent years, or maybe decades, feeling fatherless, cynical, unmoored. We were told to reach out to our government, grab hold, and it would pull us up out of the swamp. Instead it often turned, slithered, and bit us on the hand. The old rope and snake trick, in reverse.

Invariably we perceive our ongoing lives through the filter of this shared history, as if faded Kodak slides were somehow projected directly onto current events. All that we know about Watergate and the subsequent cover-up toddles into the voting booth with us thirty years later; our experience with Vietnam—whether we fought, protested, or stood on the sidelines paralyzed by confusion—shapes our vision of every new military adventure the Washington yahoos dream up; and the tragedy of 9/11 at the World Trade Center, the Pentagon, and in the Pennsylvania field down the road from where I live, will color wide swatches of our world for who knows how long.

We have double vision: what we see and what we expect to see, one scenario overlapping the other, until we aren't sure which is which.

And to compound our confusion, we live now in an increasingly virtual world, where words are detached from meanings and images digitally altered. Each major and minor moment in our collective lives, whether a war, a natural disaster, an avian flu, or a celebrity divorce, is now packaged and spun—*predis*torted before we even get the chance to project our individual prejudices upon it and misperceive it through our own inadequate lens.

No wonder so many Americans seem content to look the other way or simply shut their eyes. The world stopped making sense around the time Ronald Reagan stepped out of the movies and invaded Grenada.

So, given that I don't see clearly—that in fact, my vision is even more distorted than most (more on that later)—it makes some odd sense that I would write a memoir. I was there, after all; I misperceived it with my own eyes.

Or maybe this isn't memoir. Perhaps it is a generational autobiography—a chronicle of those events most responsible for twisting our collective psyche over the past forty or so years, especially for those of us who remember where we were on the day Kennedy died. The first one.

Paranoia *does* run deep, and we've been wading in it, up to our hipbones, for decades. Something's happening here, and what it is ain't exactly clear, but it seems that someone dropped acid on the observation deck of the World Trade Center, and our view has been topsy-turvy ever since. The folks at Three

Mile Island may have avoided a meltdown, but many of us weren't so lucky.

The walrus *was* Paul.

William Carlos Williams, the poet, once said, "Look . . . we're human beings—we're looking for company, and we're looking for understanding: someone who reminds us that we're not alone, and someone who wonders out loud about things that happen in this life, the way we do when we're walking or sitting or driving, and thinking things over."

He was explaining the appeal of Frank Sinatra, believe it or not, and, yes, Old Blue Eyes figures into this story too, but not quite yet.

For the moment I'll just pretend William Carlos was talking about me, or at least about what I'm trying to do here, as I lean on my red wheel barrow, glazed with white chickens, exploring "Lumpy" Brannum, Frank Zappa, and Baba Ram Dass. My aim is to reassure you, the reader, that you're not alone. Or maybe to reassure myself.

Or perhaps I'm just wondering out loud about things that happen in this life, the way we do when we're driving—on that road between Panic and Desire.

You'd better get in.

We're leaving any minute now.

– Don't start w/ A.

2

SON OF MR. GREEN JEANS
A Meditation on Missing Fathers

An ABC Derium   *knot*

Allen, Tim

Best known as the father on ABC's *Home Improvement* (1991–99), the popular comedian was born Timothy Allen Dick on June 13, 1953. When Allen was eleven years old, his father, Gerald Dick, was killed by a drunk driver while driving home from a University of Colorado football game.

Bees

"A man, after impregnating the woman, could drop dead," critic Camille Paglia suggested to Tim Allen in a 1995 *Esquire* interview. "That is how peripheral he is to the whole thing."

"I'm a drone," Allen responded. "Like those bees?"

"You are a drone," Paglia agreed. "That's exactly right."

Carp

After the female Japanese carp gives birth to hundreds of tiny babies, the father carp remains nearby. When he senses approaching danger he will suck the helpless babies into his mouth, and hold them safely there until the coast is clear.

Divorce

University of Arizona psychologist Sanford Braver tells a disturbing story of a woman who felt threatened by her husband's close bond with their young son. The husband had a flexible work schedule, but the wife did not, so the boy spent the bulk of his time with the father.

The mother became so jealous of the tight father-son relationship that she eventually filed for divorce, and successfully fought for sole custody. The result was that instead of being in the care of his father while the mother worked, the boy was now left in daycare.

Emperor Penguins

Once a male emperor penguin has completed the act of mating, he remains by the female's side for the next month to determine if he is indeed about to become a father. When he sees a single greenish white egg emerge from his mate's egg pouch, he begins to sing.

Scientists have characterized his song as "ecstatic."

Father Knows Best

In 1949 Robert Young began *Father Knows Best* as a radio show. Young played Jim Anderson, an average father in an average family. The show later moved to television, where it was a substantial hit.

Young's successful life, however, concluded in a tragedy of alcohol and depression. In January 1991, at age eighty-three, he attempted suicide by running a hose from his car's exhaust pipe to the interior of the vehicle. The attempt failed because the battery was dead and the car wouldn't start.

Green Genes

In Dublin, Ireland, a team of geneticists has been conducting a study to determine the origins of the Irish people. By analyzing segments of DNA from residents across different parts of the Irish countryside, then comparing this DNA with corresponding DNA segments from people elsewhere in Europe, the investigators hope to determine the derivation of Ireland's true forefathers.

Hugh Beaumont

The actor who portrayed the benevolent father on the popular TV show *Leave It to Beaver* was a Methodist minister. Tony Dow, who played older brother Wally, reports that Beaumont didn't care much for television and actually hated kids.

"Hugh wanted out of the show after the second season," Dow told the *Toronto Sun*. "He thought he should be doing films and things."

Inheritance

My own Irish forefather was a newspaperman, owned a popular nightclub, ran for mayor, and smuggled rum in a speedboat during Prohibition. He smoked, drank, ate nothing but red meat, and died of a heart attack in 1938.

His one son—my father—was only a teenager when his father died. I never learned more than the barest details about my grandfather from my father, despite my persistent questions. Other relatives tell me that the relationship had been strained.

My father was a skinny, eager-to-please little boy, battered by allergies, and not the tough guy his father had apparently wanted. My dad lost his mother at age three and later developed a severe stuttering problem, perhaps as a result of his father's sharp disapproval. My father's adult vocabulary was outstanding, due to his need for alternate words when faltering over hard consonants like *b* or *d*.

The stuttering grew worse over the years, with one noteworthy exception: after downing a few shots of Canadian whiskey my father could muster a stunning, honey-rich Irish baritone. His impromptu vocal performances became legend in local taverns, and by the time I entered the scene my father was spending every evening visiting the working class bars. Most nights he would stumble back drunk around midnight; some nights he was so drunk he would stumble through a neighbor's back door, thinking he was home.

Our phone would ring. "You'd better come get him."

As a boy I coped with this embarrassment by staying glued to the television—shows like *Father Knows Best* and *Leave It to Beaver* were my favorites. I desperately wanted someone like Hugh Beaumont to be my father, or maybe Robert Young.

Hugh Brannum, though, would have been my absolute first choice. Brannum played Mr. Green Jeans on *Captain Kangaroo*, and I remember him as kind, funny, and extremely reliable.

Jaws

My other hobby, besides watching other families on television, was an aquarium. I loved watching as my tropical fish drifted aimlessly through life, and I loved watching guppy mothers give birth. Unfortunately guppy fathers, if not moved to a separate tank, will often come along and eat their young.

Kitten

Kitten, the youngest daughter on *Father Knows Best*, was played by Lauren Chapin.

Lauren Chapin

Chapin's father, we later learned, molested her, and her mother was a severe alcoholic. After *Father Knows Best* ended in 1960,

Chapin's life came apart. At sixteen she married an auto mechanic. At eighteen she became addicted to heroin and began working as a prostitute.

Masculinity

Wolf fathers spend the daylight hours away from the pack— hunting—but return every evening. The wolf cubs, five or six to a litter, will rush out of the den when they hear their father approaching and fling themselves at him, leaping up to his face. The father will back up a few feet and disgorge food for the cubs, in small, separate piles.

Natural Selection

When my wife, Renita, confessed to me her desire to have children, the very first words out of my mouth were, "You must be crazy." Convinced that she had just proposed the worst idea imaginable, I stood from my chair, looked straight ahead, and literally marched out of the room. This was not my best moment.

Ozzie

Oswald Nelson, at thirteen, was the youngest person ever to become an Eagle Scout. Oswald went on to become Ozzie Nelson, the father in *Ozzie and Harriet*. Though the show aired years before the advent of reality television, Harriet was indeed Ozzie's real wife, Ricky and David were his real sons, and eventually Ricky and David's wives were played by their actual spouses. The current requirements for Eagle Scout make it impossible for anyone to ever beat Ozzie's record.

Penguins, Again

The female emperor penguin "catches the egg with her wings before it touches the ice," Jeffrey Moussaieff Masson writes in his book *The Emperor's Embrace*. She then places the newly laid egg on her feet, to keep it from contact with the frozen ground.

At this point both penguins will sing in unison, staring down at the egg. Eventually the male penguin will use his beak to lift the egg onto the surface of his own feet, where it will remain until hatching.

Not only does the penguin father endure the inconvenience of walking around with an egg balanced on his feet for months on end, he will also forgo food for the duration.

Quiz

1. What is Camille Paglia's view on the need for fathers?

2. Did Hugh Beaumont hate kids, and what was it he would rather have been doing than counseling the Beav?

3. Who played Mr. Green Jeans on *Captain Kangaroo*?

4. Who would you rather have as your father: Hugh Beaumont, Hugh Brannum, a wolf, or an emperor penguin?

Religion

In 1979 Lauren Chapin, the troubled actress who played Kitten, had a religious conversion. She credits her belief in Jesus with saving her life. After *his* television career ended, Methodist Minister Hugh Beaumont became a Christmas tree farmer.

Sputnik

On October 4, 1957, *Leave It to Beaver* first aired. On that same day the Soviet Union launched Sputnik I, the world's first artificial satellite. Sputnik I was about the size of a basketball, took roughly ninety-eight minutes to orbit the earth, and is often credited with escalating the Cold War and launching the U.S.-Soviet space race.

Years later, long after *Leave It to Beaver* ended its network run, a rumor persisted that Jerry Mathers, the actor who played Beaver, had died at the hands of the Soviet-backed communists in Vietnam. Actress Shelley Winters went so far as to announce it on the *Tonight Show*. But the rumor was false.

Toilets

Leave It to Beaver was the first television program to show a toilet.

Using Drugs

The presence of a supportive father is essential to helping children avoid drug problems, according to the National Center of Addiction and Substance Abuse at Columbia University. Lauren Chapin may be a prime example here. Tim Allen would be one, too. Fourteen years after his father died at the hands of a drunk driver, Allen was arrested for dealing drugs and spent two years in prison.

I also fit the gloomy pattern. Though I have so far managed to avoid my father's relentless problems with alcohol, I wasted about a decade of my life hiding behind marijuana, speed, and various hallucinogens.

Vasectomies

I had a vasectomy in 1994.

Ward's Father

In an episode titled "Beaver's Freckles," we learn that Ward Cleaver had "a hittin' father," but little else is ever revealed about Ward's fictional family. Despite Wally's constant warning—"Boy, Beav, when Dad finds out he's gonna clobber ya!"—Ward does not follow his own father's example and never hits his sons on the show. This is an example of xenogenesis.

Xenogenesis

(zen'u̱-jen'u̱-sis), n. Biol. 1. heterogenesis 2. the supposed generation of offspring completely and permanently different from the parent.

Believing in xenogenesis—though at the time I couldn't define it, spell it, *or* pronounce it—I changed my mind about having children about four years after I walked out on my wife's first suggestion of the idea.

Luckily this was five years before my vasectomy.

Y Chromosomes

The Y chromosome of the father determines a child's gender, and it is unique in that its genetic code remains relatively unchanged as it passes from father to son. The DNA in other chromosomes is more likely to get mixed between generations, in a process called recombination. What this means, apparently, is that boys have a higher likelihood of directly inheriting their ancestral traits.

Once my wife convinced me to risk being a father—this took many years and considerable prodding—my Y chromosomes chose the easy way out: our only child is a daughter.

Maria, so far, has inherited many of what people say are the Moore family's better traits—humor, a facility with words, a stubborn determination.

It is yet to be seen what she will do with the negative ones.

Zappa

Similar to the persistent "Beaver died in Vietnam" rumor of the late 1960s, Internet discussion lists of the late 1990s were filled with assertions that the actor who played Mr. Green Jeans, Hugh "Lumpy" Brannum, was in fact the father of musician Frank Zappa.

Brannum, though, had only one son, and that son was neither Frank Zappa nor this author.

Too bad.

3

DOUBLE VISION
DOUBLE VISION

"You see *what?*"

My mother lifts her foot from the accelerator, shifts it over to the brake, and the family Chevy veers to the curb, as if pulled by some unseen gravitational force. I am six or seven years old, stretched out on the large backseat.

"I see two of everything," I tell my mom.

Though I no longer remember what errand we were running that summer afternoon in the early 1960s, I clearly remember the moment when I made this confession. I remember where we stopped: 22nd and State. I remember that a telephone pole loomed just outside the car window, right along the curb. The pole, scorched by sunlight and stippled with tar stains and nails, seemed out of place on the treeless street.

My mother pauses long enough to digest my words, jerks

the Chevy into park, then turns in her seat. "You see two of everything?"

"Yeah."

"All the time?"

"Yeah," I tell her. "Pretty much."

Doctors over the years have been consistent in their diagnosis. I have diplopia, better known as double vision. In normal vision—binocular vision—both eyes focus on an object, and the image from each eye is fused into one orderly picture. My eyes don't do that.

When I focus on an object, whether a few inches or a few hundred feet beyond my nose, I see two of that object, the twin images side by side, about a half inch or so apart. One image is a fraction higher than the other. And recently I've begun to notice that the colors are slightly different—my left eye wants to go sepia.

I can't place when my eyesight went haywire in this fashion. Perhaps at birth. Perhaps when I was scalped by a hurled rock at age five. I remember garnering the same sort of stunned reaction from my mother when I walked into the living room one April afternoon, blood streaming down my forehead, and announced calmly, "I think I need a band aid."

My eyesight seemed typical enough, the way things were supposed to look, until that day I told my mother. Her shock made me realize how peculiar my vision really was.

"Can you fix it?" I asked an ophthalmologist once.

"We could fit you with special glasses," he said, "but the lenses would be thick, like the bottoms of Coke bottles." He made a gesture with his thumb and index finger, indicating lenses nearly a half-inch wide.

"Oh," I answered. "Coke bottles?"

"Yeah," he said, "and even then it might not fix the problem."

I was a young man, five feet and eleven inches of doubt and

uncertainty, not anxious to look any more awkward than I supposed that I already did.

"Have you learned to adjust?" the ophthalmologist asked.

"Pretty much."

"Then really I'd leave it alone."

When I tell friends that I have double vision, the normal reaction is a quick, uncomfortable laugh. Then a pause. Then, "You're kidding, right?"

I'm not kidding.

Those who don't have this condition seem consistently hard-pressed to believe me.

"How do you drive?" my friends ask.

I can almost hear the tumblers rolling in their brains—*click, click, click, ping*—as they sort this new information: *I was in a car with Dinty just yesterday. My God, I could be dead. Okay, first things first: don't ever get into a car with this guy again. Better yet, wait until he's completely off the road before you get into a car with anyone. Look out, he's got a knife. He's cutting into his smoked mozzarella chicken breast. How does he know that's a chicken breast and not my arm? This is dangerous.*

I can drive.

I cut my own meat, thank you.

I stroll easily down the street without regularly ramming into strangers. I even play tennis, though my return of serve deteriorates when the ball arrives with too much speed.

The human brain, an extraordinary organ, deals pretty well with diplopia. My eyes register two mismatched images and send the faulty signal forward without proper correction, but the brain knows instinctively that this version has to be wrong and suppresses one image over the other. Most of the time I'm oblivious to this constant process of suppression—the brain makes the adjustment for me, without need for discussion.

If I wish, however, I can take control of the process, even

alternate between images—suppressing the left image or the right—at whim.

In other words, like so many people, I see only what I want to see.

Human perception is little more than a funhouse mirror covered with dust and jelly. We see *something* reflected in that mirror, but goodness only knows how close that something is to the truth.

This is the best-case scenario.

But I am the worst case, or at least a *worse* case. I misperceive twice. Double Double vision vision. My defective perception creates *two* funhouse mirrors, smeared with all the usual jam and grime, but one slightly off to the side, a bit higher in the vertical plane, tending toward sepia. No wonder I inevitably lean toward the comic twist. Nothing is as it seems anyway. Look how quickly it all reverses.

Then again—and this is only occurring to me as I round the age of fifty—if *none* of us sees accurately, maybe I've been at an advantage all of these years. At least *I* know that I am not seeing clearly. There is less temptation to take the world, and one's ideas about it, too seriously when you understand right up front that what you see, or think you see, is mere approximation.

Nonetheless, I still remember the day, and remember it clearly—the summer afternoon that I revealed my double vision. I remember the telephone pole along State Street, just outside the backseat window of my mother's car. I remember the shape of the tar stains, the pattern of nails. Parched brown wood against a hot white sky.

"You see what?" my mother asked.

I see that pole.

Both of them.
Both of them.

4

SON OF RICHARD M. NIXON

The halls of Saint Andrew's Catholic Elementary always seemed dark. When I think back to those days, moving cautiously from room to room, scurrying from the cafeteria to the small basement library, the corridors remain ominous and shadowed—somewhere no child would wish to linger a moment more than absolutely needed.

Perhaps that was intentional.

It was in one of those gloomy hallways, on a Friday in November, 1963, waiting for my chance at the boy's lavatory, lined up in perfect single file behind a dozen of my male classmates, with our uniform blue shirts and clip-on navy ties, that I heard the PA system crackle to life.

"This is Sister Mary Rita. I would like your complete attention."

The public address system was piped only into the classrooms, not into the dim corridors, so the nun's shrill voice came across as an eccentric echo.

"President Kennedy was shot today in Dallas, Texas, and his injuries are very grave. Let us say a silent prayer asking God to grant him a quick recovery."

My classroom teacher, plump Sister Eugene, grabbed immediately for her oversized rosary and began clacking her way through a torrent of distressed and fruitless Hail Marys. Perhaps some of the boys around me prayed also, but all I really noticed was nervous shuffling and a few frail noises of concern.

Five, maybe ten seconds after the echo of Sister Mary Rita's announcement drifted into silence, I turned to the boy directly behind me in the lavatory line, Mike Timko.

"You know," I whispered, "Nixon did it."

To say that mine was a Kennedy family would be a considerable understatement. JFK whistle-stopped through our small Lake Erie city during the campaign's earliest days, and my thirtysomething mother signed on immediately as a hardcore Kennedy activist. Our basement was crammed with buttons, brochures, and banners, and for a few months it seemed as if all adult conversation centered on the young Jack.

I distinctly remember one cardboard box on a basement table packed full of promotional 45 RPM records, a classic Frank Sinatra ditty slightly reworked to become a Kennedy theme song:

> Everyone wants to back—Jack
> Jack is on the right track
> 'Cause he's got high hopes
> He's got high hopes

It took no time at all for my Mom's own high apple-pie-in-the-sky hopes to join themselves directly to Kennedy and his alluring vision of a confident new country called Camelot. His message was irresistible.

So was the messenger. I suspect that my mother, like so many women of that time, had fallen in love with young Jack. Here was one honey-voiced Irishman who would never let her down.

Mom moved to Erie, Pennsylvania, midway through World War II, hired to edit a small corporate magazine. She was just out of high school in central New Jersey, where she had been editor of her school paper—they called her "Scoop" in those days—and the new position was a considerable opportunity. She imagined the plum job would be the first step on an upward ladder.

But the former editor returned just as soon as the war ended, and in a common scenario of that time he was granted his old position back, just as if he had never gone. My mother was let go.

She met my father soon after. She married him partly because he was charming—a curly-headed young man with a shy smile—and partly out of economic desperation. She was out of work. My father, she understood, was studying hard to one day enter medical school. He would be a doctor, and with him her future would be set.

I can only imagine the degree to which my mother must have yearned for security. Her parents divorced when she was still a toddler, and both died before she reached her early teens. The circumstances of her father's passing have always been murky. One relative insists that he jumped in front of an elevated train in Chicago; another maintains that he was pushed. Whatever the case, he was only thirty-four years old, and somehow no one kept a copy of the death certificate or an obituary.

Five years later my mother's mother died as well, and again no one seems able to offer a particularly coherent account. Mom was sent to live with her Aunt Marcella. Marcella had children of her own and a small house, so my mother and her sister Ruthie slept in the attic.

Here is how my mom told it, seventy years later:

"After the funeral no one ever spoke about my mother again. My aunt was wonderful to us, simply wonderful, but she never talked about my parents or about anything that had happened. Of course that's how they did things in those days. No one said a word."

Shortly after Sister Mary Rita's grim announcement, the school day ended. I walked the half mile home and crept through the back screen door, already concerned.

My mother was watching television, of course. Everyone was. President Kennedy had died. She looked up from the screen and told me to throw some clothes into a paper bag. "Grace is coming by to pick you up."

I spent the ensuing long weekend with my father's sister—my Aunt Grace—watching the unfathomable events unfold on a small blue television in the back sunroom, dipping absent-mindedly into communal bowls of buttered popcorn.

Oswald had killed Kennedy.

Jack Ruby had killed Oswald.

There were horses, right on the streets of Washington.

The world, it seemed, would never be the same.

And for me, in fact, it wasn't. That November weekend marks the moment that my mother irretrievably changed, at least in my perception. I was oversimplifying perhaps—seeing a complex world through the incomplete understanding of a child—but this is what I knew:

I would wander in after school to find Mom upstairs in bed, behind a tightly closed door. I would knock—"I'm home"—and carefully enter. The shades would be drawn; a damp washcloth would be draped over my mother's forehead, shielding her eyes from whatever dim light found its way into the room. My impression was that she had been there, just like that, since I'd left that morning with my book bag and baloney sandwiches.

"How are you?" she would ask, sometimes not even lifting her head.

"I'm okay," I would reassure her.

"Oh, that's good."

There was little use pretending, but we still did.

The clearest memory I have of my father from those years, just after Kennedy's assassination, is the sound of the back screen door squeaking open. We would be in our beds—me, my mother, my two older sisters. Mom would have left a pot on the stove with her husband's dinner.

Forty years later I can easily recall the sound of that back screen, of my father pulling out his chair, of the refrigerator opening, of his fork scraping against the plate. These midnight sounds meant my father had arrived home safely and all would be well.

He *could* have been a doctor; he certainly had the brainpower. But my father's college career was cut short when Holy Cross tossed him out for running a saloon in his dorm room. He tried again at his hometown college, but couldn't seem to make it to his classes. My father was a gifted Irish tenor, and often when he sang in bars the drinks would flow for free. He found the attention, and the whiskey, irresistible.

Then he went off to war. His exceptional test scores and interest in medicine qualified him to work on a hospital evacuation ship, treating the casualties, or just keeping them alive, as they steamed back across the Atlantic.

When the war ended for my father, he met my mother and convinced her that he was about to start anew. But children arrived, money became an issue, and a friend found him a job as a pit mechanic at the local Chevy dealer, where he remained for most of his working life.

It is an all-too-common story of the postwar era, but it is my story too.

In November 1963 no one offered any sensible explanation—not Cronkite, not Brinkley, not my dear Aunt Grace. Oswald was an evil person. For some reason he hated Kennedy. He had, at one point, lived in Russia. That's all we seemed to know.

An eight-year-old wants answers, though, for everything, but especially for something so horrible and enormous. How could one man destroy the dream of an entire nation just by shooting from a sixth-story window? How did Ruby kill Oswald so easily, right on television? I required some better reason why evil had won that day in November. I wanted to know why my mother had sent me away. Most of all I wanted someone to explain my father.

Even at that age I knew what was normal and what was not. And the Friday afternoon trips to Dailey's Chevrolet to snatch my father's paycheck before he had a chance to cash it himself; the late-night phone calls announcing "your father's here, better come get him;" the way my sister Susan would tiptoe downstairs after Dad finally made it to bed to ensure that the stove was not left on—none of that was normal.

But in those days no one said a word.

My mother left my father two years after Kennedy died.

I woke one morning, wolfed down my frosted flakes, skittered off to school. In the afternoon I was called unexpectedly out of a geography lesson, passed through the dim hallways, met my mother in Sister Mary Rita's office.

"We're moving," she told me.

Earlier that day, after my father went to work, according to a plan known only to a few key conspirators, our entire household, top to bottom, had been packed into a moving van. All that my mother left behind was a single bed, some blankets, a chair, one set of silverware and dishes, a pot, a frying pan, and my father's clothes. Presumably she left him a note as well.

Mom led me to the car, explained all of this before turning

the ignition, and I sat mutely as we drove four miles uptown to our cheerless one-floor apartment in an unfamiliar neighborhood. I shuffled up the broken sidewalk and opened the front door, where my sister Sally was busy scrubbing the wooden floors with Murphy Oil Soap.

I still hate that smell.

There were other things I hated about those next eight months: my new school; my new teacher; my new friends, who taught me how to shoplift items I didn't need or even want; the dreary people in the apartment upstairs; and most of all, being alone while my mother went off to a new job and my sisters disappeared with new boyfriends who had cars.

Each Friday night Dad would drop in to politely deliver a small check for child support. The shock of our relocation had been enough to sober him for the first time in his adult life, and oddly he seemed so different now that I didn't know what to say or how to talk with him.

"Do you like your new school?" he would ask me.

"Sure," I would lie. "It's just great."

In less than a year we were moving back to the very same house we had left. My father had been persuaded to find a room elsewhere.

I was roaming the gloomy hallways of St. Andrew's again, making life unpleasant for the nuns. My mother rotated through a series of part-time jobs, and in between she could be found back in bed with a wet washcloth blocking the sunlight from her eyes. Our neighbors, boys older than I, went off one by one to Vietnam. My father resumed drinking. My sisters, understandably, fled the moment they finished high school.

I was alone now, in that house full of ghosts, stranded in my mother's somber world. Like my mother, I began to feel the heaviness, a formless cloud that varied in size and shape, but never seemed to lift entirely. What use *was* there in high hopes? Kennedy was dead. And then his brother. Why have dreams and splendid expectations? They would only be dashed.

My own days became predictable: staring out a window, ignoring hollow facts etched onto a classroom blackboard, wondering what I had done to deserve the life that clung to me like fog. The parish priest listened to my cheerless confessions every Friday, but didn't seem to care. The teachers didn't care either; my grades were good enough.

Mom began dating a man whose wife had died a few years earlier, so most evenings I would sit alone, cross-legged on the floor, and watch other families on television—families that fought, misunderstood, then made it all up to one another in thirty easy minutes.

The shows were filled with people coming in and out of rooms, in and out of doorways, always bursting with conversation. The opposite of what my life had become. No one came in and out of our doorway. There was no one I could engage in conversation, and worse, no one I really wanted to talk to.

All the important people had gone away.

Except one person, of course.

On the morning of November 7, 1968, I sat alone, pouring sugar onto my cereal, listening to a man on the portable Zenith television tell me that Richard M. Nixon had squeaked out a narrow victory overnight, and he, finally, would be going to the White House.

Nixon *had* done it.

I was right all along.

5

THREE BAD TRIPS, 1968–77

Nixon Nixon bush league President
this is a populous hymn to you and yours
And I begin with your face and come back to your face
Lawrence Ferlinghetti, *Tyrannus Nix*

The Boy Reporter

Around the time Richard Nixon won the White House with his
secret plan to end the war, I was entering high school, about four
years away from hearing my own draft number called. In Mark
Kristof's dingy garage, someone handed me my first joint.

Nixon's trip to power started off well, but soon unraveled
like a Greek drama, thanks to covert bombings, steady leaks,
and inept plumbers. By the time the Watergate scandal came to
dominate the nation's airwaves, I had found my calling.

Bob Woodward and Carl Bernstein, rebellious sons in khaki pants and rumpled Brooks Brothers shirts, rolled up their sleeves and took on the potent patriarch. The symbolism was too strong for me to resist, and in my second year of college I threw myself headlong into reporting for the campus newspaper. Right across from the newsroom was the office of the College Republicans, and they were so shifty, so smug, so thin-lipped and acned, it was obvious they were up to no good.

The budding Bernsteins of the *Pitt News* would sneer at the wannabe Haldemans each time we passed in the narrow third-floor hallway, and in my mind every one of my scornful expressions, every haircut missed, every joint rolled and savored, was a blow against Nixon, Rebozo, Agnew, and all that gang.

Soon I fell into a double life of sorts—wearing rumpled pin-striped shirts as editor in chief of the campus newsroom, sending freshman reporters off to cover the latest student government scandal, penning scathing editorials about fraternity hypocrisy or Marxist professors denied tenure, while at the same time growing increasingly dependent on grass and speed, sleeping through my morning and (eventually) afternoon classes, and spending whatever free time I could carve out of this schedule engaged in late-night, chemically-altered card games hosted by my new best buddies, Hagen and DiBartello.

DiBartello dealt more than cards. At times, when he or Hagen thought the cops were onto them, one or the other would show up on my apartment doorstep with a steamer trunk. "Here, hide this for me." Then a laugh. "No one's ever going to suspect you."

The World Trade Center

I overslept the morning of my college graduation and missed the ceremony, but later that month two old friends, Mac and Jim, met me in New York City to celebrate.

We dropped acid, strolled through Chinatown around dinner-time, gawked at pallets of wide-eyed carp—broad mouths gaping for a last breath. A caged chicken on Mott Street kickboxed for kernels of corn. I dropped dimes into a slot, and the chicken started kicking just for me. We marveled at the glazed ducklings crucified in restaurant windows. Slithering tubs of iced eels. The white knight was talking backwards. Alice was ten feet tall.

The sky above lower Manhattan seemed pea green, and as we traveled further down the island the streets grew otherworldly. New York was unaware of who we were, but in our minds we owned the narrow island, and as dusk fell our world seemed indescribably promising and alive.

And then we turned a corner.

In front of us stood the World Trade Center, perhaps a quarter mile off. Somehow I had forgotten it would be there. The twin towers climbed into the pea green sky as if by magic, and we three young Jacks knew at once that we had to ascend the glimmering beanstalks, toward whatever destiny.

We stumbled into an elevator, giggled like odd little monkeys as the floor went soft beneath our feet. We were airborne.

Moments later we gazed over the edge of the observation deck, as wide-eyed and gape-mouthed as Chinatown fish. Our sensations were on the very edge of tolerable. Color, sound, the cold metal of the railings, all manner of odors blowing over from Hackensack, the sense of being *so* high, literally—all of this threatened to take us apart, wrest away our self-control.

But it didn't.

Until I became separated.

Mac and Jim had wandered around a corner, laughing at some private joke, and I found myself alone in a gaggle of strangers, a shifting herd of blonde, blue-eyed tourists with cameras, USA T-shirts, and guidebooks in hand. They were smiling, pointing, remarking on all that could be seen from the observation deck, but I couldn't understand a goddamned syllable of it. I couldn't process one word.

My memory of this particular moment remains razor sharp: I was suddenly convinced that all ability to process language, to understand simple speech, had been lost, and I was scared in ways that were entirely new to my experience. How could I ask for help if I couldn't even manage words? How could I find my friends? How would I ever get down the elevator alone? My panic ran 110 stories deep.

More tourists gathered, and conversations grew louder, more baffling. I was on a Tower of Babel, witless and confused.

All of this took only minutes, most likely, but it seemed like hours, and with every uttered phrase that I could not decipher, my terror only worsened, until I literally curled up into a fetal shape against one of the Plexiglas observation windows and tried my best to disappear.

That's where my pals found me.

"What's wrong?" Jim asked, a wide grin on his bearded face. He was still riding the happy high.

"I can't understand a word," I whispered, pointing to the people bunched all around me, still consulting their guidebooks, spouting gibberish. "I'm losing it, really."

"You can't understand them?" Jim asked. His smile never wavered.

"Not a word."

"Not a word?" Jim repeated.

Mac started laughing. Jim too. They laughed as if this were the happiest moment of our celebratory adventure. As if I were the funniest fellow they had ever met.

Just at that moment it hit me—I had understood Jim. His words were clear. His questions had made perfect sense.

And I understood Mac, too, when he said, "You idiot."

"What?" I asked.

"It's a tour group, man."

"A tour group?"

"Yeah. A tour group. They're all from Sweden."

The Flood

Two months later, one early morning in late July, twelve inches of rain pounded the hills and mountains of central Pennsylvania, resulting in the third major flood to hit Johnstown in eighty-eight years. The Conemaugh, the Little Conemaugh, and the Stonycreek rivers all rose above their banks and funneled deadly walls of water downstream, until seven dams broke and my phone rang.

I was sound asleep, of course, in my ratty little Pittsburgh apartment, still suffering the aftermath of an all-night binge —speed, grass, maybe mushrooms, I don't honestly remember—but I could barely speak, my mouth was so dry.

"There's a flood," a man said, "in Johnstown. You have a car, right?"

Just prior to my college graduation I had been hired by United Press International (UPI), the wire service, but wasn't scheduled to actually start work until mid-August. Now Johnstown was underwater, and they needed extra hands.

The voice on the phone was John Rutherford, bureau chief. "Drive over this morning and see if you can get into the area," he instructed. "Then find a phone and call me."

I slithered out of bed, brushed and showered, put on my rumpled pinstripe shirt, and hustled to my putty-colored '72 Datsun. I took a few hits off a spent joint in the ashtray, just to clear my head.

The car never made it to the National Guard checkpoint outside of the flood zone, because the engine died an hour or so later in the small town of Armagh. Still, I was close enough to hitchhike, and did.

The next two days were spent wandering through rubble and mud, phoning in occasional eyewitness accounts to UPI's Pittsburgh office, where someone folded my words into the official statements issued out of Harrisburg and Washington. Roughly eighty-five people were dead or missing, and property damage exceeded two hundred million dollars. I mainly followed other reporters around, big shots from the national papers, and if they wrote something in their little notebooks, I wrote it down too.

Eventually my bureau chief called me home, and some National Guard officer, taking pity on the stranded kid-reporter with no car, offered to haul me back to Pittsburgh in a four-seat helicopter. I managed to smoke my last joint behind a building just before the chopper embarked.

And soon I was airborne again. As we climbed above the Laurel Highlands, skimming just over tree level, I inched closer and closer to the open doorway. The thwack of the rotors and the rushing air transported me. I wasn't the lost and lonely boy-reporter. I was a gunner in Vietnam.

Rat a tat. Rat a tat.

The trees were filled with evil people trying hard to bring me down.

6

QUESTIONS AND ACTIVITIES BEFORE CONTINUING

1. Which of the following would you advocate as an appropriate replacement father for the author of this memoir:

   A. Hugh Beaumont
   B. Hugh Brannum
   C. A big plastic baggie of aromatic marijuana
   D. Twenty-five years of cognitive therapy
   E. All of the above

2. Dinty has been dating Camille Paglia for three years. Paglia, though, decides to break up with Dinty after he cheats on her with Yoko Ono. "You're a drone," Paglia says, "and I hate you!" What Paglia doesn't know is that Yoko lured Dinty into the indiscretion because she was jealous of Camille's penetrating cultural criticism. After

the breakup Dinty is consumed with guilt, smokes dope alone in his room, watches old television programs in his underwear, and persistently calls Camille to beg for her forgiveness.

Yoko, for her part, tells Dinty that she's glad he feels guilty for hurting Paglia. "This is your fault," she says. "You're a very, very bad man."

Yoko is using _____ as a defense mechanism.

A. denial
B. projection
C. performance art
D. kickboxing

3. Mark these statements true or false:

___ Frank Zappa died in Vietnam.
___ Jerry "the Beav" Mathers married Tricia Nixon.
___ Xenogenesis occurs when an emperor penguin gives birth to hungry little wolf cubs.
___ The author of this quirky memoir exited childhood depressed, self-pitying, and badly in need of a working alarm clock.

4. Write a brief essay where you explore various connections between the following: (A) rumpled Brooks Brother pin-striped shirts, (B) Richard M. Nixon's disgrace and fall from power, (C) baseball, (D) hot dogs, (E) mescaline, and (F) the family Chevrolet.

part two. **PARANOIA**

7

INTRODUCTION
Imagine That

Hello! Thanks for calling the Panic and Desire Psychic Hotline today. This is Tricia at extension 1341. You'll want to remember that number. What is your name and date of birth?

Dinty. August 11, 1955.

Dinty, I'm going to do an in-depth reading for you, and I will be relying quite heavily on my telepathic impressions to guide us through our psychic journey. It is important that you be able to clear your mind and concentrate on the reading with me. Can you do that?

Sure.

Dinty, why don't you get yourself a pen and paper to copy down my callback number in case we are disconnected. It's 1-800-555-9999, and, once again, my extension is 1341. This is my direct number with the Panic and Desire Psychic Hotline, and you can reach me anytime just by calling it.

Great.

Now you'll want to take down some notes about your reading, because we're going to cover a lot of important territory. Dinty, I'm going to start with my intuitive impressions. Please ask any questions you have as I go along, and I'll make sure that everything is as clear to you as possible. Do you have any questions to start out?

Yes, Tricia, I have one question: What the hell am I doing calling a telephone psychic?

That's an excellent question, Dinty. In fact, right now I'm sensing an especially strong "need to know" on your part, a healthy sense of purpose and mission.

Am I right about that?

Maybe.

That's wonderful. I already feel that this conversation is going to be of great use to you.

Now let me tell you some more of what I'm sensing here. Your early years were filled with fear and disappointment, much of it related to a broken family. As a child you felt quite vulnerable—

Imagine that.

And you watched a lot of television.

Everyone watched a lot of television.

Yes, but there's more. What you saw on television didn't match up with the world that you inhabited. Your parents didn't live up to the expectations created by the mom and dad on *Father Knows Best* or *Leave It to Beaver*, and your life wasn't nearly as fun or funny as the lives of Wally and the Beav. Meanwhile, on the evening news, you witnessed death and destruction, dishonesty and peril—

Um, no offense Tricia, but you're basically describing 90 percent of everyone born in the 1950s or '60s, at least everyone with a TV set in the living room. You might as well be reading from a script.

I'm sensing resistance, Dinty. It's important that you release any feelings of doubt or skepticism you have about this phone call—or your hesitation could significantly block the psychic pathways between us. Do you understand me?

Yeah, I understand, but here's another question: how much is this costing?

Dinty, the first three minutes are entirely free, and there is a modest and reasonable charge beyond that. Let's not worry about the cost right now, but instead let's try to fully focus on the images that are coming into our shared mind space this morning.

I'll give it another minute.

I'm sensing that the Kennedy assassination was a tough time for you. Your world began to seem precarious. No longer safe. Unseen forces threatened from every corner. Innocence and optimism were hard to sustain—

You're still describing a lot of people, Tricia.

And I sense, too, that as soon as you heard of President Kennedy's death, you blamed my father.

Excuse me?

My father. You saw my father as the center of all that was evil, and later, when he was elected president, you—

Your father?

This is Tricia. Tricia Nixon. You knew that, right?

You work for a psychic hotline?

Times are tough. Chuck and I have kids in college.

Richard Nixon is your father?

In many ways he's the father of us all, isn't he Dinty? He defined our formative years. Now let's move on. Are you still there?

Barely.

Great! That's good to hear. I'm sensing another image now. You are atop a large building—a skyscraper—the Empire State Building maybe, and you feel disoriented—

The World Trade Center.

Yes. And you seem lost. You seem as if you can't take in the multitude of sights, sounds, and sensory inputs; you can't make sense of what is happening or construct a version of reality that allows you to move forward—

I was on LSD.

No, I'm no longer talking about on top of that building. I mean right now. Right here. At this point in your life, as you pick up the phone and call me. You seem lost. You seem overwhelmed. You don't know what to do next.

Keep talking . . .

One by one, Dinty, the symbols of safety and security came apart in your life. Your father could not be counted on to protect you or your family. Your mother receded into her own shuttered bedroom. The president was killed. And then his brother. And Martin Luther King Jr. How does that song go? "Only the good die young?" And we were at war, of course, and it turned out that the government lied to us about Vietnam and Laos and Cambodia. And then that horrible Watergate mess. You know my father didn't really know as much as people—

But he lied.

Yes, he did lie, and that's unfortunate. But you can't blame everything—the nation's failures, your personal failures, the next ten years of your life—on one man's tragic imperfections and some third-rate burglary. You have some responsibility here, obviously. You took your lack of trust in certain people and conveniently converted it into a lack of trust in everyone, including yourself. You smoked pot from morning to night, avoiding your own doubts and misgivings. Julie and I avoided marijuana, thank goodness. Nasty smelling stuff. And anyway the Secret Service would have been on us in a second. I hated those guys, thinking they were so cool behind the sunglasses. A lot of them were creeps. But anyway, back to you: so you left home at eighteen and essentially created a world for yourself not so different from the one that you fled, because at least you knew how to survive there. Adults were not to be trusted, disaster was around every corner, get your playtime in now because who knows what problems—

I began projecting. The old rope and snake.

Sometimes you were projecting. Sometimes hallucinating.

And I'm doing it again, aren't I? I look at George W. Bush, and I see your father. I look at Karl Rove, and he might as well be Haldeman . . . The war in Iraq is just another quagmire—

Dinty. Those things haven't happened yet.

Oh.

It's not quite 1980.

It isn't?

You're not done screwing up.

I'm not?

Not even close.

But if you can see into the past, Tricia, then you can see into the future, and you can warn me right now. What mistakes should I avoid? What do I do with all this panic? Where are the ropes, Tricia? Where are the snakes?

(Beep.)

Tricia?

(Beep.)

Tricia?

Dinty, that tone you are hearing means the amount you've authorized on your credit card for this call is about to expire, but we aren't done exploring these very important issues, are we? I sense that we are definitely close to some significant realizations. So Dinty, as one of my special customers, I want to give you a unique toll-free number to call, allowing you future readings at the discounted rate of only ninety-nine cents per minute.

Please write this number down.

Do you have a piece of paper handy?

Dinty? Are you still there?

8

BASEBALL, HOT DOGS, MESCALINE, AND CHEVROLET

Thus it came about that, one bright May morning, I swallowed four-tenths of a gram of mescalin dissolved in half a glass of water and sat down to wait for the results. **Aldous Huxley,** *Doors of Perception*

"A large pale blue automobile was standing at the curb."
Unlike Aldous Huxley's dream car, mine was black—jet black, convertible, with rounded fenders, and a silver Indian chief on the hood. My dream car sat in the woods, abandoned. We found it rusting, hemmed in by trees and brush, with no easy answer as to how it had arrived. Maybe fifteen years earlier there had been a path or dirt track, some way to drive a car into this dense urban thicket, but we couldn't see that now. Four crew-cut boys in cutoff jeans—wheeling our bikes through damp woods in

search of anything to divert our boredom—all we could see was an inexplicable circumstance, pure mystery.

It was midsummer, and the weeds and ferns were so plush underfoot that we didn't need our kickstands. We simply let our Schwinns and Huffys fall onto the soft green carpet, then we bounded forward on foot, descending on the abandoned car as if it were the long-lost grail. I remember, even now, the intense radiated heat of the dark metal baking in the July sun; can still recall the smell of rubber tires and some peculiar odor coming off the cloth seats. If I close my eyes I can see the torn ragtop and the loose piles of broken glass scattered everywhere. The car, I believe, was a Pontiac from the mid-1940s. My ten-year-old mind had great difficulty comprehending this unexpected discovery—someone abandoning an entire car. *An entire car?*

At that point I was holding onto everything in my brief life: bottle caps, baseball cards, small bits of oddly shaped stone. Yet someone had left behind a car, lost track of a full-sized automobile. It made no sense.

Perhaps that's why Tommy Mucciarone refused to approach. Tommy just glanced fretfully over his left shoulder while the rest of us, the boys on the Schwinns and Huffys, yanked at the oxidized wipers, searched for the missing cigarette lighter, picked through the rubble and trash of the floorboards for coins, maps, clues, whatever little thing we could find.

Tommy, no doubt, was anxious that the owner might return. He understood—we all understood, from the layers of rust and the thick growth of weeds perforating the floorboards—that this hulk had been here for a decade or longer. But the owner might still come back.

This was a car after all.

We would've come back, had it been our car.

"At the sight of it, I was suddenly overcome by enormous merriment."

Occurrences are not alone and we are not apart from that which does occur if only when the stars are out and waters

rise to lunar songs of times before they knew the moon
was earth to men in solemn cubes of blueish light on
evening rides with relatives and closer friends than even
neighbors are
Again
Times then came when old men drank in musty bars
and cherry bombed the bathrooms until laughter struck
the night and whiskey breaths puffed home to lukewarm
meals and upset women's hearts until morning drenched
the sky and woke the men who panted off to work
Again
And times then came when women drove in drunken
fear through whitened roads of shining hopes and banks
of snowy fantasies until the metal touched and ripped and
ran and wandered to a formal place where pistoled men
write funny words and listen to their radios so they can
drive you home in emblemmed cars so neighbors can peek
out and wonder where the lady had gone wrong.

I wrote that breathless bit of prose roughly twenty-five years
ago; banged it out on a Royal typewriter while tanning shirtless
on the lawn behind my apartment building. I was stoned when
I wrote it. High as a kite.
  I think it shows.

**"What complacency, what an absurd self-satisfaction beamed from
those bulging surfaces of glossiest enamel!"**

For the first three decades of my life, the automobile and inebri-
ation were fairly well connected. I'm not bragging, understand.
Not even close. This is just how it was.
  My first automobile memory was the inspiration for what-
ever you want to call that piece of writing above. Lyric essay?
Prose poem? A cry for help?
  I recall, quite clearly, careening through a blizzard one Christ-

mas Eve, my mother at the wheel. No one should have been driving that night, given the poor visibility, but more to the point, my mother was abundantly drunk—so bombed that she eventually scraped the front fender of our family Chevy across the side panels of two or three parked cars. I was seven, maybe eight. "Don't worry," my mother kept telling me. "I'm all right." But she wasn't, and she knew it.

We were a block or two from our house when it finally dawned on Mom that scraping metal to metal against a line of parked cars was not acceptable, no matter how much snow was falling, or what the holiday. Her response—and even if you are horrified for the little boy that I was, you have to see the humor in this—was to drive another two miles, entirely out of her way, straight down snowdrifted West Eighth Street to the City Hall police station. Once there, she turned herself in.

The officers behind the desk, perhaps already caught up in their own Christmas Eve revelry, seemed to find my mother's predicament amusing. I don't remember this part quite so well, but I'm guessing they took down the pertinent information. Or maybe they didn't. It was Christmas Eve after all.

What I do remember is that eventually they drove me and my mother home in a black-and-white cruiser with chains on the tires.

"Man had created the thing in his own image—"

Some years later, I turned sixteen. My friend Peter had a Volvo—or rather, his father had a Volvo—and we spent most weekend evenings pretending this bit of Swedish engineering was an enchanted carpet. We would fill the Volvo's interior full of sweet marijuana smoke and cruise the wide, green boulevards of our lakefront hometown as if on some magical mystery tour.

The smoke gave our world a pleasant, surreal quality. It served as antidote to edgy teenage boredom. It blocked out the trouble all of us were having at home. It connected us with our older brothers and sisters, the Woodstock kids. It was an all-purpose high.

Sometimes Peter, Danny, and I would veer into the Kmart parking lot, finish a joint or roll up a new one, and stumble inside to watch the night owls shop under the strange fluorescent lights. The shoppers seemed so oddly significant examining boxes of detergent in the unnatural glare.

We would giggle a lot.

Then we would drive some more.

The first car I ever owned was a putty-colored '72 Datsun. I bought it for four hundred dollars in Squirrel Hill, my favorite Pittsburgh neighborhood. I hadn't yet learned to drive a standard shift, though the car I purchased had one, so my dope-dealer friend Hagen drove me around for the first few days. Eventually—yes, of course, we were taking hits from his improvised pipe—he taught me to drive the car myself.

My second car was a 1966 vw Beetle, with an engine not much larger than what you might find in a midsized snowblower. The 12-volt electrical system could barely power the headlights—they often dimmed when the car accelerated. There was no heat.

One late December afternoon in 1983, returning home from a Christmas Holiday break, I took my Beetle onto the Pennsylvania Turnpike. As chance would have it, a massive ice storm moved in quickly behind me, covered every surface with a dangerous, glassy sheen. But I didn't stop. I was determined to get home.

In those days smoking marijuana while driving was standard practice. The dope made long car trips palatable, passed the time quickly, helped me stay at my most alert—there was no end to my rationalizations for what had, at that time, become a clear addiction. But the fact is this: I almost never drove any distance without my pipe and baggie at my side.

So I smoked a little weed as the ice storm started, a bit more as the ice storm worsened; soon enough the drive became an endless, fantastic ordeal of slipping, sliding, and trying to avoid stalled automobiles blocking the lanes. What should have been a four-hour drive stretched into twelve, then thirteen hours. The little vw was steady and reliable—an advantage of the rear engine—until midnight, or around then, when I came to a hill just below the Kittatinny Tunnel. The road was a sheer sheet of ice at this point. I went nowhere. My tires merely spun in place.

Soon I spotted the huge headlights of a tractor-trailer coming up in my rearview mirror, and thought, "Oh God, I've done it now."

The lights kept coming.

I kept spinning.

The tires whined.

Nothing.

Let's step back a minute:

> The vw Beetle wasn't called "bug" for nothing. It was small, eminently squashable.
> The Pennsylvania Turnpike is notoriously dangerous, even in good weather.
> This was a *severe* ice storm.
> And I was high, as usual, in only partial control of my reactions, reflexes, and senses. How stupid could I have been?

The truck continued forward until it made contact, but it didn't hit me so much as nudge me—quite gently, given the vehicle's enormous size. The unseen pilot slowly and deliberately placed the tractor-trailer's front end directly onto the rear of my tiny lump of car, locked his front bumper onto the vw's engine compartment, and pushed me up the hill into the tunnel, where the pavement was dry and traction was again possible. Then he slowed enough for me to move forward on my own power.

He was either being nice, or he needed to be somewhere on schedule and wanted me out of the way.

"—or rather in the image of his favorite character in fiction."

In his futuristic novel *Brave New World*, Aldous Huxley spends much of the first chapter narrating the manner in which electrical shocks are administered to infants. These shock treatments are a form of mental preconditioning, intended to make the "khaki babies" averse to flowers. Why flowers? Love of nature, the Director of the Hatchery explains, doesn't do enough to encourage citizens to consume both "manufactured articles" and, as he puts it, "transport."

In Huxley's fiction mechanical transport is sacred. "Our Lord" is replaced with "Our Ford." Crosses have their tops lopped off to resemble Ts. (As in Model Ts.) "Ford's in his flivver," the Director remarks at one juncture. "All's well with the world."

Huxley's State wants its citizens to purchase vehicles and fill the storage compartments with costly gear—mountain bikes; Polartec fleece; Global Positioning Systems; two hundred dollar poly/nylon, micro ripstop shell, super-wicking sleeping bags—before heading into the mountains.

I've modernized the list, of course, because Huxley is not around to do so himself. Nor is he able to witness all of those suv commercials punctuating our nightly television. "Who needs legs?" these ads tell us. "Load it all up, and *drive* to the top of the mountain!"

You are what you own.

Clearly the State has won.

"I laughed till the tears ran down my cheeks."

Julian Heicklen, a professor emeritus of chemistry at Penn State University and perennial candidate for local office on the Libertarian ticket, regularly issues statements such as, "It is immoral to arrest someone for owning a vegetable. We have the right to keep and bear vegetables."

The vegetable Heicklen wants us to keep and bear is marijuana. A few years back, Heicklen set his lawn chair in the middle of a main State College intersection and handed out flyers that read, "Hello! I am Professor Julian Heicklen, and I love our children. I want to do everything I can to protect them, and that is why we are blocking traffic today. Automobile accidents are responsible for more child deaths each year than any other accident and most natural causes. We want to outlaw the automobile. Anyone owning an automobile should be imprisoned."

He gave reasons, including these:

> Unlike marijuana, which has never been responsible for a single death in all of human history, the automobile kills 44,000 people each year in the United States alone. It maims and injures many more people.
>
> Unlike marijuana, which is not criminogenic, the automobile is highly criminogenic. It leads to manslaughter, reckless endangerment, driving under the influence of alcohol, speeding, and parking violations. It also is used in the commission of crimes, such as arson and armed robbery.

Heicklen also pointed out that the automobile has no clear "medicinal use" and that people "deprived of their cars display irritability and irresponsibility."

In short, he posited, the car is a recreational drug, and we are clearly addicted.

"We re-entered the house. A meal had been prepared. Somebody, who was not yet identical with myself, fell to with ravenous appetite. From a considerable distance and without much interest, I looked on."

In *The Doors of Perception*, Huxley's readers will find a passage—one that follows closely after the sentences I've used as section headings in this chapter—in which Huxley expounds further on his mescaline-fueled car trip: "And then, abruptly, we were at an intersection, waiting to cross Sunset Boulevard. Before us the cars were rolling by in a steady stream—thousands of them, all bright and shiny like an advertiser's dream and each more ludicrous than the last." He goes on: "Once again I was convulsed with laughter. The Red Sea of traffic parted at last, and we crossed into another oasis of trees and lawns and roses. In a few minutes we had climbed to a vantage point in the hills, and there was the city spread out beneath us. Rather disappointingly, it looked very like the city I had seen on other occasions."

Huxley was disappointed, I suspect, because what he really wanted was transcendence, some sort of mystical vision. But he wasn't approaching the spiritual.

In fact, let me tell you from my own experience:

He was merely stoned.

"When the meal had been eaten, we got into the car and went for a drive."

Here is the rest of *my* dream-car story:

The boys with the Schwinns and Huffys didn't sit in the abandoned Pontiac that afternoon, although that is exactly what you might expect four young boys to do. We crawled in and out and over the rusting shell, but we carefully did *not* lower our bottoms onto the sour, scratchy seats.

You see, we could too easily imagine that something awful,

something dangerous, had occurred on those seats, or why else would the car have been left to rot? Maybe booze was involved. Maybe something worse.

We were as naive as boys of our age are meant to be—knew little about drinking, drugs, or Huxley's warnings about mechanization, and the inherent danger of a society based on the shallow consumption of manufactured goods—but we could sense power. We knew it resided here, in this object, this magical abandoned automobile. We sensed the energy in this odd hunk of metal. Rusted, stripped, the engine long dead, yet even this forsaken wreck held a promise we could not yet fully identify.

You will have a car someday, it promised. You will be an adult, and all of what is hinted at here will be a part of your life. You will hold this enormous power in your hands, and use it, or abuse it, exactly as you wish.

9

I believe in everything until it's disproved. So I believe in fairies, the myths, dragons. It all exists, even if it's in your mind. **John Lennon**

Number 9, Number 9, Number 9 . . . **Unidentified sound engineer,** "Revolution 9"

The night the Beatles appeared on the Ed Sullivan Show—February 9, 1964—I succumbed like everyone else. Cuban missiles and Cold War had defined our lives for too long. America needed a diversion.

Enter Ringo.

9

In my bedroom on Ninth Street, my transistor radio under the pillow, I eagerly anticipated each new single:

"Can't Buy Me Love"
"Eight Days a Week"
"Do You Want to Know a Secret?"
Boy, did I ever.

9

For instance, where was Paul?

In 1968, soon after Martin Luther King Jr. and Bobby Kennedy were gunned down, a Detroit disc jockey received a phone call advising him to listen closely to the endings of certain Beatles songs and to play other tracks in reverse.

He did just that, and discovered John muttering "I buried Paul" at the conclusion of "Strawberry Fields Forever." In addition, the line "Paul is dead man, miss him, miss him" could be heard—if you wanted badly enough to hear it—in the space connecting "I'm So Tired" to "Blackbird."

And on the cover of *Abbey Road*, Paul was not only out of step with the others, but barefoot.

That's how the British bury their dead, someone suggested.

9

On "Revolution 9," the disconcerting eight-minute sound collage on the second record of *The Beatles* (aka *The White Album*), a male voice repeats the words "number nine." Played in reverse, the brief snippet sounds eerily like someone straining to say "turn me on dead man."

The song scared the crap out of me, in either direction. John and Paul had been trotting out a lot of peculiar ideas in that period, but the bizarre cacophony of nightmarish noise on "Revolution 9" went beyond anything I could explain or had ever expected.

Truth be told, I was less frightened by the notion that the Beatles had put the reverse message onto the album intentionally, than by the more startling idea that this dark message may have ended up on the disc through some other means—that the words "turn me on dead man" were *not* intentional.

First Jack, then Martin, then Bobby.

It was not too much to imagine—not for me at least—that imperceptible evil was moving, somewhere, underneath the visible surface of the world.

Or in the grooves of a record.

Evil itself pressed into a black vinyl disc.

9

Charles Manson believed it.

Convinced that the ninth chapter of the biblical book of Revelation spoke to him directly, he supposed, as well, that the dissonant chords of "Revolution 9" were part of the equation, somehow completing various long-awaited biblical prophecies.

Revelation's chapter 9 speaks of a bottomless pit out of which locusts come forth. "And they had hair as the hair of women, and their teeth were as the teeth of lions." Manson understood these locusts to be the Beatles, four mop-headed angels of the apocalypse.

Verse nine of the ninth chapter reads, "And they had breastplates, as it were breastplates of iron; and the sound of their wings was as the sound of chariots of many horses running to battle."

The breastplates, Manson somehow decided, were the Beatles' guitars.

9

Manson had long been obsessed with a coming race war, believing it would begin when poor black folks stormed into rich white neighborhoods like Beverly Hills and murdered the wealthy. The series of events Manson envisioned beyond that moment make little sense, unless you believe in underground caverns filled with lizard people, but Manson was able to convince a handful of troubled followers, including Tex Watson.

Just after midnight on the evening of August 9, 1969, four of Manson's devotees butchered five people in Beverly Hills, including actress Sharon Tate. When he entered Tate's home, Tex Watson is reported to have said, "I'm here to do the devil's business."

9

John always had a thing about the number nine.

He was born on October 9.

His son Sean was born on October 9.

Brian Epstein, the Beatles's manager, first saw the group on November 9.

John met Yoko on yet another November 9.

For a while in his youth, John lived at 9 Newcastle Road.

Liverpool has nine letters.

9

"Nine seems to be my number, so I've stuck with it," John once explained, "and it's the highest number in the universe; after that you go back to one."

9

The Beatles drifted back to one—back, that is, to solo careers—pretty soon after the "Paul is dead" debacle petered out. By 1971 John had moved to New York, aligning himself with the growing peace movement. Within weeks he was meeting with Jerry Rubin and other members of the New Left, planning an antiwar Woodstock.

The following February a secret memo was sent to Richard Nixon by Senator Strom Thurmond, pointing out the danger Lennon's activism might cause to Nixon's reelection and suggesting a termination of Lennon's visa. But Thurmond was late to the party.

J. Edgar Hoover's FBI had been watching Lennon for years.

9

They should have been watching Arthur Bremer.

Bremer was attending Nixon rallies with a gun in hand, waiting for a chance to shoot Tricky Dick of Yorba Linda. But security was too tight, so Bremer eventually turned to Alabama governor George Wallace, a candidate for the Democratic presidential nomination, gunning him down at a 1972 campaign rally and leaving him partially paralyzed.

9

Only later, when the Nixon tapes were released, did we learn of Nixon's private reaction to the Wallace shooting. Nixon looked immediately for some way to earn partisan points from the tragedy and advocated leaking rumors that the gunman was tied to the Democrats. "Just say he was a supporter of McGovern and Kennedy," Nixon instructed his aides. "Just put that out . . . say you have it on unmistakable evidence."

9

In February of 1974, Samuel J. Byck, distraught that Nixon had ignored struggling small businessmen, hatched a plan to hijack a commercial airliner and coerce the crew to crash into the White House. Byck went to the Baltimore/Washington International Airport, forced his way onto a Delta flight by fatally shooting an airport policeman, and ordered the crew to depart.

After the crew informed him that they could not go anywhere without removing the wheel blocks, Byck shot them.

He then realized there was no one to fly the plane.

So he shot himself.

This was twenty-seven years before 9/11.

The plane was a DC-9.

9

At various points in history the number nine has been considered ominous. For instance, in the year 999, many Europeans gave away property and forgave debts, believing the world was on the verge of a Second Coming. On New Year's Eve 999, there are reports that people literally died of fright.

9

Nine is also mathematically unique.

Multiply any whole number (other than zero) by nine, and the sum of the digits will be, or eventually come to, nine (e.g., $21 \times 9 = 189; 1 + 8 + 9 = 18; 1 + 8 = 9$).

Reverse the number of the original product, and the number you get (in this case 981) will also be a multiple of nine.

9

There are nine muses.

9

My favorite line from the song "Revolution 9," by the way, was not the one spoken by the sound engineer, but one spoken by Yoko, John's muse:

"If you become naked," she whispered, never completing the thought.

I was in ninth grade.

It seemed like an invitation.

9

Ninth grade was also the first time I tasted marijuana smoke.

9

Paul Krassner, underground magazine editor, was getting high around the same time, with Lynette "Squeaky" Fromme.

Krassner had been corresponding with Charlie Manson, already in prison for life, and Manson suggested that Krassner hook up with Squeaky, one of his devoted followers. Krassner, "on an impulse," bought some LSD from the man who would later become Baba Ram Dass and took it along. He dropped the acid with Squeaky and her roommates, Brenda McCann and Sandra Good.

"Squeaky told me lots of Charlie stories and I began to understand his peculiar charisma," Krassner writes of his meeting. During the visit Sandra Good asked Krassner to relay a message to John Lennon.

He should get rid of Yoko, she said, and stick to "his own kind."

9

The same year that Nixon was forced to resign his office—on August 9—John Lennon ominously predicted, "Everybody loves you when you're six foot in the ground."

Soon after, Squeaky Fromme showed up at a rally to see President Gerald Ford. She was carrying a .45-caliber automatic pistol with four bullets in the clip, but Fromme was wrestled down by the Secret Service before anyone was shot.

I watched the news that night and thought Squeaky was cute.

9

Lennon's ninth solo album was released that same year, in the ninth month. On it was the song "#9 Dream," which some say predicted John's own assassination. "Took a walk down the street," he writes, only to hear "Somebody call out my name."

9

Musicologists joke about a "ninth symphony syndrome."

Beethoven died in 1827, after writing his Ninth Symphony.

The following year Franz Schubert died as well, after his ninth was completed.

The Czech composer Antonín Dvořák attempted to trick fate by calling his Ninth Symphony *Number Five*, but he still expired in 1904—before completing his tenth.

Gustav Mahler tried the name-change technique as well, naming his Ninth Symphony *Das Lied von der Erde*. He attempted to complete a tenth, which he labeled as his ninth, but died before he could finish.

Composer Jean Sibelius, on the other hand, stopped writing symphonies after his eighth was completed—and lived another thirty-three years.

9

Around the time of Squeaky's failed attempt on Gerald Ford, Martin Scorsese was busy shooting his signature film, *Taxi Driver*. The movie chronicles antihero Travis Bickle and his growing obsession with a twelve-year-old hooker, played by Jodie Foster. Bickle stalks a presidential candidate with gun in hand but is repeatedly blocked by the candidate's security men. He must quickly change his plans, so instead he kills a pimp and ends up being portrayed by the media as a crusading folk hero.

Screenwriter Paul Schrader based the character on the man who shot and paralyzed Wallace—Arthur Bremer.

9

Travis Bickle was a loner, ruled by irrational delusions and fantasies of greatness.

So was Mark David Chapman.

In his teens Chapman heard voices. "I used to fantasize that I was a king, and I had all these Little People around me and that they lived in the walls," he would explain later. "And that I was their hero and . . . and I was on TV every day . . . and that I was important." When he wanted to entertain the imaginary little people in his bedroom walls, Chapman would give concerts for them, often playing Beatles records.

Like Manson, Chapman came to believe that certain albums held secret messages. Chapman was a fan of Todd Rundgren and presumed that the title of Rundgren's 1980 album—*Deface the Music*—was a signal meant for him.

9

On December 8, 1980, Chapman waited outside the Dakota apartment building for John and Yoko to return from a recording session. When Lennon exited his limousine, Chapman called out his name—"Mr. Lennon"—then fired four pistol shots, killing the former Beatle. Afterwards, Chapman waited for the police, pacing and reading his copy of *The Catcher in the Rye.*

9

The number nine is ruled by Mars, the god of war.
Nine is associated with metal—missiles, knives, guns.

9

Across from the Dakota that evening, thousands of mourners began immediately to congregate. Among them was John Hinckley Jr.

Hinckley had seen the movie *Taxi Driver*—fifteen times—and had begun to imitate Travis Bickle's preference for fatigue jackets, army boots, and peach brandy. He also developed an obsession with Jodie Foster, the child-prostitute in the film, and began to stalk her, fantasizing about various ways to capture her attention, including possibly hijacking an airplane.

Instead, Hinckley settled on assassination as his best strategy to win Foster's heart, and on March 30, 1981, fired six times at President Ronald Reagan outside of the Hilton Hotel in Washington DC.

In Hinckley's hotel room, police found a John Lennon calendar and a paperback copy of *The Catcher in the Rye.*

9

After that event, producer Julia Philips reported running into Hollywood bigwig Bert Schneider at a party and joking about the connection between Reagan's shooting and the film she had helped produce.

"See, *Taxi Driver* wasn't such a bad movie," Philips quipped.

"If it was really great," Schneider reportedly answered, "Hinckley would have killed him."

9

Had Reagan died, he would have continued an unusual numerical string.

Starting in the mid-1800s, every president who was elected in a year ending in a zero had died in office. William Harrison (elected in 1840) died of pneumonia. Abraham Lincoln (1860) was assassinated, as were James Garfield (1880) and William McKinley (1900). Warren Harding (1920) died of a heart attack, and Franklin Roosevelt (1940) of cerebral hemorrhage.

John F. Kennedy, of course, was elected in 1960.

9

George W. Bush became president in 2000 but has not died in office.

Perhaps this is because Ronald Reagan broke the curse.

Or perhaps, as some still believe, because Bush was not *actually* elected.

9

The family of would-be Reagan assassin, John Hinckley, has longstanding ties to the family of George W. Bush. Hinckley's brother, Scott, in fact, had plans to dine with Neil Bush, George W.'s brother and former campaign manager, on the day after Hinckley shot Reagan. The dinner was cancelled.

Asked later if he had ever met would-be-assassin John Hinckley, Neil Bush answered, "I have no idea. I don't recognize any pictures of him. I just wish I could see a better picture of him."

9

If you lighten the hair a bit and change the eyebrows to seem a bit less sinister, that may as well be a picture of me, as I looked back in the early 1980s.

Like Hinckley, Chapman, Lennon, and Manson, getting high was the best part of my day. About the same time that Hinckley was watching *Taxi Driver* obsessively, I was dropping acid in Chinatown, obsessing over kickboxing chickens. My friends and I wandered google-eyed through lower Manhattan, until we ended up on top of the World Trade Center.

It was a bad trip.

9/11

But not nearly as bad as the eleventh day of the ninth month of the year 2001, when two terrorist-controlled planes destroyed the twin towers.

The towers, side by side, looked like the number eleven.

The first plane to hit the towers was American Airlines flight 11.

After September 11 there are 111 days left to the end of the year.

New York City has eleven letters.

So does the name George W. Bush.

11

So it is either nine or eleven we should fear most.

Or the Bush family.

Or Beatles records, played backwards.

11

Or it could be me.

My name has eleven letters, and I was born on August 11.

I once saw George W. Bush waving in my direction from the back of a presidential limousine.

There was a rose bush in my family's backyard.

On Ninth Street.

The rose bush was covered with beetles.

The walrus was Paul.

Goo goo ga joob.

11

Nine, nine. Nine. Nine. Nine. Eleven. Nine eleven. Eleven. Nine.

Are we seeing just too many coincidences?

Maybe not.

Mathematicians assert that even this many concurrences are simply inevitable. "We're awash in a torrent of names, numbers, dates, addresses, acronyms, telephone calls, e-mails, calendars, birth dates," Temple University professor John Paulos explains. "In reality, the most astonishingly incredible coincidence imaginable would be the complete absence of all coincidences."

Or in other words, the phrase "World Trade Center" has sixteen letters.

Bush has four.

Lennon never met Kennedy, and Chapman never met Oswald.

The Catcher in the Rye has eighteen letters, and Manson has only six.

But we don't see that.

We only see the repetition of details that seem to fit.

9

In fact our basic biological programming—behaviors that go back to the earliest humans and our animal cousins—favors the propensity to see patterns. Statistician Persi Diaconis (thirteen letters) believes that humans are hardwired to overreact to patterns and repetition. Actually, being a bit paranoid can be an advantage for survival.

"It goes back to primitive man," Diaconis tells us. "You look in the bush, it looks like stripes, you'd better get out of there before you determine the odds that you're looking at a tiger. The cost of being flattened by the tiger is high."

And the cost of fleeing is low.

We live longer, it seems, if we imagine the worst.

9

And of course conspiracy theories can be oddly reassuring.

Given the two options as to how the words "turn me on dead man" appeared on "Revolution 9"—because John Lennon put them there, or for reasons none of us can comprehend—there is good reason the latter scared me far worse than the former. No one wants to think that bad things derive from purely unseen forces, that some cloak of evil exists well beyond our perception. Such a belief would be too frightening. It can actually feel *better* to believe that the CIA programmed Charles Manson.

9

Another example:

If you rearrange the letters in Osama Bin Laden, you can form the phrase "A damn alien SOB."

Well, if Osama *were* an alien—like, from Pluto—then we'd have an easier answer to why he has done what he has done. He came from outer space.

9

Along the same lines of logic, if the entire canon of unfortunate global events—assassinations, oil crises, climate changes, levee breaches—could be laid at the door of nefarious cartels with far more power than we can even imagine (e.g., Opus Dei, the Elders of Zion, Halliburton), then we as individuals would be off the hook.

How nice to be off the hook, excused any moral or political responsibility for the crisis at hand.

And being off the hook has an additional benefit: we are freed from having to participate in any painful remedy. We can over-consume like hogs. Cheat on our taxes. Drive our SUVs.

Someone else is to blame.

9

It took seventeen years and countless court cases, but eventually the Federal Bureau of Investigation (twenty-eight letters) was forced to release John Lennon's files.

One portion of the dossier listed the lyrics to the song "John Sinclair," lyrics that had been "classified" since 1971 despite the fact that they were available in any record store, on John's album cover. Another section of the top secret FBI file detailed the incendiary slogans regularly squawked by a parrot belonging to one of John's antiwar friends. A third section contained the FBI's top secret appraisal of the musical talent of Lennon's wife.

Yoko, a field agent dutifully reported, "can't even remain on key."

11

I, for one, am grateful that the government kept such close tabs on Yoko's uncertain vocal ability, because she, after all, was the one who broke up the Beatles.

Moreover, her family played an integral, behind-the-scenes role in Japan's attack on Pearl Harbor.

You didn't know that?

Yoko Ono was born into one of Japan's most dominant lineages, an important power behind the throne. Her paternal great-grandfather, Atsushi Saisho, descended from a ninth-century emperor, and her maternal grandfather, the billionaire Zenjiro Yasuda, headed up one of Japan's richest business cartels, both before and after the war. Yoko attended school with Emperor Hirohito's sons, Akihito and Yoshi.

Rearrange the letters of Atsushi Saisho, by the way, and you get "Ah so, U.S.A. is shit."

9

Could it be *any* more obvious?

The hell with Osama Bin Laden.

Where was Yoko when those damn planes hit the towers?

10

It was a bright, cold day in April, and the clocks were striking thirteen.

Dinty W. Smith, his chin nuzzled into his breast in an effort to escape the vile winds of West Philadelphia, slipped quickly through the glass doors of the Wharton Ministry for Collateral Synergy, though not quickly enough to prevent a swirl of gritty dust from entering along with him.

The hallway smelt of New Coke.

At one end a colored poster had been tacked to the wall. It depicted simply an enormous face: a kindly Irish uncle, handsome in a Hollywood sort of way, and winking.

Underneath, a caption:

BIG RONNY IS WATCHING[1]

---

1. With apologies to George Orwell, from whom much of the story of Dinty Smith has been stolen.

The year 1984 found me editing grant applications, research proposals, and client reports for one of the numerous think tanks affiliated with the University of Pennsylvania's Wharton School of Business. My route here had been decidedly haphazard.

After skipping out of journalism to make documentary films, I determined that filmmaking was tedious and hard, not glamorous or easy. So I quit that too, and for months amused myself by writing and rewriting the first ten pages of a hideous novel while mopping floors to pay the rent. All I remember now about the failed book is that Ted Kennedy was a secondary character, and at about page eight I ran out of plot.

As luck would have it I was mopping floors in the dormitory of a small college that housed an experimental dance-theater company. Danceteller merged acting and modern dance into surreal stage presentations and survived (just barely) by traveling up and down the East Coast in a dilapidated van playing one-night stands. The inescapable truth about dance companies is that they are almost always desperate for male performers, so soon enough I had convinced the artistic director to make me part of the troupe. My specialty was rushing out onto stage like a beast and throwing myself onto the floor.

This lasted about four years, before I upped and searched for something with even less of a future. Which brought me to Philadelphia, where one day, while waiting tables at the White Dog Café, I asked two customers dressed in business attire if they knew where "I might find a real job."

One of them smiled, perhaps admiring my bald gumption, and asked, "Well, what can you do?"

The other just stared into his mock turtle soup.

Luckily the one who took the bait was the research center's director, and when I claimed that I could both write and edit, listing some real and imagined credits in journalism and grantsmanship, he brought me in for an interview. And somehow I got the job.

The world of Wharton seemed entirely Orwellian to me. Newspeak was the unique jargon of corporate consulting that allowed someone with an MBA to earn $250,000 per year for stating the obvious to those who were disinclined to listen. My coworkers were, by and large, smart and nice and diligent, yet I would sit through daily meetings and want to scream—*You are using all of these big words just to mask the fact that you aren't saying a damn thing!*

But that would be a thoughtcrime.

If this is what *real* grown-ups do to make money, I counseled my late-blooming, still dope-addled, twenty-nine-year-old, unmotivated self, then I'd better investigate food stamps.

Inside the Ministry of Collateral Synergy, a fruity voice was reading out a list of figures related to a landmark empirical field comparison of xenogenetic management strategies in the soft drink sector. The voice came from an oblong metal plaque like a dulled mirror that formed part of the surface of the right-hand wall.

Dinty turned a switch and the voice sank somewhat, though the words were still distinguishable. Someone was explaining that Michael Jackson had just set his own hair on fire.

Dinty moved over to the window.

Outside, even through the shut windowpane, the world looked cold. Down Market Street little eddies of wind were whirling cheesesteak wrappers into spirals, and though the sun was shining and the sky a harsh blue, there seemed to be no color in anything, except the posters that were plastered everywhere. Big Ronny, the kindly Irish Uncle, gazed down from every commanding corner.

There was one poster on the office building immediately opposite:

JUST SAY NO, it was captioned.

Another, just above the first, read,

IT'S MORNING IN AMERICA.

A third, pasted on the side of a Hunan lunch truck, proclaimed,

STAR WARS IS PEACE.

But in the end, the job I despised so much became a blessing in clever disguise.

Like Orwell's diligent Winston, I started scribbling my own thoughts on Wharton company time, hoping the odd new Apple Macintosh computers didn't project both ways like telescreens. My random notes and observations turned into humorous stories, and those humorous stories showed up in the local *City Paper*.

For the first time in ten years, since I had bailed out on journalism, I felt like a writer again. But you can't write stoned—at least *I* couldn't with any clarity or sense—and suddenly there was something I wanted more than to stay chemically removed from every strange or disturbing thought springing into my head. I wanted to capture those strange and disturbing thoughts, and I wanted to remember them the next day.

Desire began to overtake panic.

An odd feeling indeed.

11

QUESTIONS AND ACTIVITIES BEFORE CONTINUING

9. Fill in the blanks from the following list of choices:

Because Paul McCartney's desire to keep the Beatles together as a group ran counter to John Lennon's interest in avant-garde artistic exploration, _____ was _____.

A. Yoko . . . a conniving bitch
B. J. Edgar Hoover . . . pretty in pink
C. Squeaky Fromme . . . freckled, elfin, and cute as a button
D. the walrus . . . Paul

9. Both of author Dinty W. Moore's parents were orphaned. Little Orphan Annie was orphaned, too, and had a dog named Sandy. Sandy is not a real dog, but a cartoon dog. Cartoon dogs are incredibly cute. Based on these facts we can conclude that:

A. Squeaky Fromme was a dog.
B. Little Orphan Annie tried to shoot Gerald Ford.
C. The author is not real, but a cartoon character.

9. What do you suppose Moore is saying in the ten chapters you have read so far? Is he suggesting that everything we think of as real is instead a mere product of our mental projections, and thus reality does not exist? Or is he suggesting that there *is* a reality, but our tendency to project our preconceptions onto every object and incident around us keeps us from being able to see that reality with any accuracy? Write an essay in which you argue that Moore is not real either.

9. Or simply imagine that you have written the essay. Was it (A) brilliant (B) fairly good, or (C) pretty much a complete waste of your time?

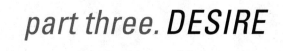

part three. DESIRE

12

INTRODUCTION
Why Oprah Doesn't Call

Consider these factors:

a history of family alcoholism;
a father who is seldom sober and almost never around;
Mom, depressed and defeated, retreats to her bed;
a young man's recreational drug habit becomes, well,
    habit-forming;
the young man broods, crumples shamelessly into his own
    sick despair;
lacks any real career direction;
drives while high;
repeatedly.

We all know where that story is heading: the inevitable automobile accident—a dramatic, siren-filled, brush with violent

dismemberment along a long, lonely highway—leading to a last-minute flash of enlightened realization. Total turnaround by tourniquet. Maybe a guest spot on some popular inspirational television program.

Or perhaps a harrowing visit to drug rehab, complete with the imaginary snakes of panic slithering up padded white walls while our hallucinating narrator (James "Dinty" Frey) shouts preposterously at a towering orderly:

"You can't treat me like this. I'm the son of Mr. Green Jeans, dammit!"

However, the gods of narrative arc were not so kind to the author of this unconventional, nonsequential, generational autobiography, *aka* cultural memoir. Somehow I sidestepped the brutal catharsis leading to sudden conversion. Instead I took a few additional stumbling turns and enjoyed a lucky break here or there.

The *real* story goes like this:

I placed one foot in front of the other, just kicking the can of desire down the road.

Which isn't as easy as it seems when you see two of everything.

13

SON OF GEORGE McMANUS

We are what we pretend to be, so we must be careful about what we pretend to be. **Kurt Vonnegut,** *Mother Night*

Bringing Up Father was a popular comic strip created in 1913, but if you ask your grandparents they'll remember it as "Maggie and Jiggs." That's what everyone called it, because Maggie and Jiggs were fairly unforgettable.

George McManus's daily comic followed the working-class couple's ups and downs after they win the Irish sweepstakes. Jiggs, a stonemason by trade, didn't take well to the pampered world of chauffeurs and afternoon tea, longing instead for his old pals, familiar foods, and impromptu poker games at the corner saloon. Maggie wanted status, stability, and a reliably sober companion.

Much of the humor derives from the tension between these

competing desires. The final panel of the strip often depicts Maggie, rolling pin in hand, waiting silently behind the front door of their sparkling new mansion. Jiggs, inevitably, is sneaking home drunk, dress shoes in hand, reeking of corned beef and cabbage.

McManus's comic was an instant and enduring hit, because it worked on twin levels. The jokes were good, the characters well drawn, the situation—instant prosperity—wrought with comic possibility. But underneath the jokes the strip was sociologically brilliant, capturing precisely the passionate dreams and fears of the new immigrant working classes.

For many Irish the primary reason for coming to America was to move forward in life, but to move forward often meant moving *beyond* your own people, leaving behind what was familiar and comfortable. Songs, vaudeville acts, and other forms of popular humor poking fun at "mick on the make" were rampant at the time because they struck a deep chord.

My great-grandfather James Moore didn't win any Irish sweepstakes, but after immigrating in the late 1800s he managed to scratch his way into the middle class. He did this through real estate, marriage, or crime. I've heard all three explanations but have had little luck tracking down the truth.

My father insisted that old James was murdered by gangsters and buried under a main highway of our hometown, but Dad told a lot of stories that later turned out to be far from actual. There's an expression for this sort of blarney: Irish facts.

What is verifiable is that James Moore's only son, my grandfather Billy, lived in an grand house near the Erie bayfront, owned a popular nightclub, managed blocks of prime real estate, and was somewhere between a civic leader and a scoundrel. Like Jiggs, he traveled in "lace curtain" circles but loved nothing more than to hoist a beer or two (or six or eight) with the old gang at Sullivan's Saloon.

One of my father's favorite stories involved a high-ranking figure in the local Catholic Church. The celibate man of God would drop by the house on Friday evenings, have a drink or two in the parlor, disappear briefly upstairs, and return in civilian clothing. He was round, solid, like my grandfather, so everything fit. Both men would head to Cleveland for the evening, presumably to engage in pursuits the man found unavailable on his home turf or in his priestly collar.

My grandfather—he died seventeen years before I was born, so I rely on my father's stories and a few yellowed newspaper clippings—profited from Prohibition. He owned a fast boat, lived in a city full of Irish cops. Canada was just a quick trip across Lake Erie.

He once stymied federal agents by filling his speedboat with nuns from a local convent, ostensibly taking them on an afternoon cruise. The brides of Christ returned from Ontario with bottles of blessed nectar hidden under their full black habits. No treasury agent was going to frisk a good sister.

"Why would they go along with that?" I once asked my father. He just laughed.

The nuns were Irish. They liked a good drink too.

There's more, some of it not so amusing.

My mother was born into a family of Chicago printers, fairly well-established at the turn of the century, but circumstances unraveled when her father died. She was only eight; and barely five years later her mother died as well. Mom was raised by an Irish aunt from the less well-heeled side of the family tree.

She married my father, in part, because she believed he was the ticket to regaining lost respectability. Her new suitor was from a prominent family and, when they met just after World War II, he claimed to be headed off to medical school.

But the narrative arc was not kind to them either: unlike Maggie and Jiggs, Bill and Cathy were headed *down* the ladder of class and affluence.

My father was also orphaned young and raised by a kindly Irish aunt. Family assets were sold off one by one to finance elaborate vacations and private schools. In the end no money remained to speak of, and by the time he hit adulthood, my army-veteran father preferred hanging around the same saloons his father once frequented to the hard work of cracking open medical books.

My parents' adult lives turned out to be an ironic reemergence of the old comic stereotype: Maggie the wife hounding Jiggs to stay home, be a family man, pay attention to the children, fix the faucet, stop all that drinking with ne'er-do-well friends in low-class dives.

McManus had them nailed.

Anyone familiar with early comic strip history is perhaps well ahead of me, but for the rest of you, here's the kicker:

Though the social themes of class tension and upward Irish-American mobility found in McManus's funny paper saga connect to my kinfolk in countless ways, what ties me most directly to this comic burlesque is that Jiggs was sneaking out night after night to visit a *particular* saloon: Dinty Moore's.

My namesake was the third most popular character in "Bringing Up Father," a wiry, mustachioed, cigar-smoking scoundrel in spats and a bowler hat. Dinty not only owned the tavern that Jiggs habitually retreated to when ducking out of Maggie's society soirees, but Dinty was Jiggs's best friend, his one remaining connection to the working-class world he so badly missed.

Dinty Moore represented everything that Irish American men of that time clung to like lifelines: buckets of beer, fatty corned beef, backroom card games, coarse language, and the absence of pesky family responsibilities that tended to dictate when a man had to be home.

Not surprisingly Maggie hated the rascal, often ending the

daily comic with lines such as "I don't want you sneaking off with that Dinty Moore fellow," or "Huh! It's that Dinty again!"

So the question remains, why in heaven's name would a woman knowingly name her son after a comic strip character whose chief activity was luring respectable fellows out of their homes to drink beer and play cards? Especially given the fact that her husband stayed out night after night, drinking beer and playing cards. There's an odd one for you.

I should point out that just a week or so prior to my birth, Mom mentioned to the good priests at St. Patrick's her intention to give me the comic-strip name. The priests made it exquisitely clear that they would never baptize me under that moniker, and as a result my birth certificate and baptismal records list me as William. But my mother called me Dinty from the first second of my life, as has everyone close to me, and that's the name I live by, and how I pay my taxes.

The comic Dinty was a gentle stereotype, a wink and a nod toward working-class male camaraderie, but the case can be made that he was also a bit of an ethnic slur. The Irish were lazy, drunk, unwashed, according to prejudices of the time, and Dinty's comic character played into each of these. All in all, a great handle for a beaming boy.

Mom's usual account is that her cousin Jimmy insisted that "any Irish lad with the last name Moore" had to be known as "Dinty." Jamesy-boy, as he was called, was Mom's favorite male cousin, and he probably enjoyed a good laugh when he opened his morning paper, but this still seems a pretty weak rationale.

My best guess is that my name connects to the fact that my mother's Irishness was of great importance to her. She was only half Irish, in fact, and her father's side of the family—English and Eastern European (actual Bohemians)—seemed largely to lose interest in Mom and her sister after their father died. It was the maternal, Irish side—the O'Briens and Smiths—who became her comfort and support.

So perhaps calling me Dinty was just my mother's symbolic way of staking claim to the part of her own family that did not disappoint or abandon her.

Or maybe she had a better reason.

My father, so the story goes, could not be found high or low on the August evening that my mother went into labor, despite repeated phone calls to Mentley's Tavern, Barilla's Bar, and the Cascade Club. He had a standing agreement with his favorite bartenders to say, "Oh, Bud just left," whether Dad actually had moved on or was sitting right there.

Maybe my mother was angry, and rightfully so, since she had, after two daughters, delivered what every red-blooded American male was desperately supposed to want—a healthy, bouncing masculine child.

So, as expected, she named her pink-cheeked son William Jr., on the birth certificate at least, after his rascal of a father. And then, to make her point, she never, ever, used that name again.

14

THREE MILESTONES

1.

The Johnstown flood was my first UPI assignment, but after that I was strictly high and dry, consigned to the twelfth floor of the Manor Building in downtown Pittsburgh.

The dramatic world of wire service journalism, it turned out, consisted primarily of reading every local paper in Western Pennsylvania, rewriting human interest stories, grabbing headlines off the radio, and typing up notes phoned in by underpaid stringers. Our subscribers wanted a steady stream of news ratcheting out of the teletype machines, and UPI couldn't afford the reporting staff necessary to make that happen, so we recycled. Shamelessly.

Occasionally I got an assignment that took me out of the office, usually to one of the downtown hotels where I would sit in a gaggle of press people and ask questions of some reluctant official. I met Henry Kissinger this way, earned my fifteen seconds of fame on the CBS Evening News asking some loaded post-Vietnam question I don't even remember. I met Gerald Ford, too, and was pushed backwards into a chair by his press secretary, Ron Nessen, because I was young, obnoxious, and insistent.

Even being manhandled by the mouthpiece of the man who pardoned my antihero Richard Nixon was not enough to keep me interested, however, and truth be told, I was still smoking dope in my car before work or at lunch or whenever I could sneak down to the parking garage, which limited my energy, my focus, and—in retrospect, this was perhaps the most damaging effect—undercut my self-confidence. I was a young man going nowhere, and if you didn't believe it, you could've just asked me.

Late March, 1979, I informed my senior editor, Malcolm Hughes, that I was calling it quits. An old buddy had just graduated NYU film school and talked me into joining him in making documentary films using handheld cameras and an editing bay he installed in his attic. Using the least expensive technology available, we could knock out a thirty-minute film for about two thousand dollars, not counting six or so months of our own labor. Then we could enter these films into festivals and contests, possibly earning a top prize of five hundred dollars.

Made sense.

"Moore," my editor said, "we'd like you to stay on."

"Sorry. I'm pretty sure my mind is made up."

"What would it take? How can I convince you?"

"I've already got plans, sort of." I really liked Hughes. I hated to disappoint him. "I'm kind of obligated."

"Okay, Moore, here's what we'll do."

"Mike" Hughes stood from his desk, walked into the newsroom, and returned with the front page of that morning's *Post-Gazette*. Three Mile Island, the nuclear facility outside of Harrisburg, was suffering a partial core meltdown. Governor

Thornburgh was torn as to whether to evacuate the immediate area, a wider area that would include the state capitol, or whether he should just tell everyone within earshot to run like hell and never have children.

The story was fresh—having broken just the previous day—and was already attracting international interest.

"Moore, here is what I'm willing to offer. You stick around, I'll send you to Harrisburg this afternoon. You can make your reputation. Waddya think?"

2.

A few weeks later I relocated to a sleepy rural town in central Pennsylvania, spitting distance from the Mason-Dixon Line. My friend Jim's new wife had secured a position teaching the young women at Wilson College how to draw and paint, so that's where we started our film company.

Chambersburg had wide avenues and spotless front porches; and even a pool hall downtown. It was like a scene from *The Music Man*, except in the movie there was no character that rode his bike around and around in circles, lost and disheartened, a Kodak film canister full of marijuana in his pocket.

One day, sitting high on my bike, I glanced through a window in an alleyway and saw a young woman in a dress, the dress covered by a green-checked apron. She was thin, dark-eyed, with flowing hair, and she was setting a dining room table. I saw a male figure disappear into a doorway, presumably the kitchen.

I didn't see much more than that because the bike was coasting, just like me, but in my mind it was all clear. The woman in the window was newly married, her future settled, her young husband embarking on a stable, secure career. He was everything that I was not and would never be. She was all that I would never have.

It embarrasses me to say all of this, so maudlin and melodramatic, but the moment is true. I wore my loneliness like a badge in those days.

You couldn't have a relationship when you had so many secrets. You couldn't be good enough for someone else when you clearly weren't good enough for yourself.

I thought, *Oh, well*, and pedaled away.

3.

Three years later my father died.

I had been living with the woman in the dining room window for two years at that point, having met her by roundabout coincidence. We spent all our time together, starting about the moment I realized her roommate, the fellow she was setting the table for, was gay. Nice guy, too.

The woman in the window was sitting next to me when the call came that my father finally passed. It was throat cancer, and expected. She came with me to the funeral, and she attended the small wake and dutifully entertained embarrassed guests while I went to a back bedroom to referee a fight between my sisters over who would inherit my father's old desk.

Later that day Renita and I drove to the Lake Erie shoreline, my dad's favorite spot, and right there, both of us sitting on a big hunk of driftwood, I asked her to marry me.

Which she did.

And so it goes.

15

LEONARD KOAN

And just when I was sure
that his teachings were pure
Leonard Cohen, "One of Us Cannot Be Wrong"

The Koan

Two Buddhist monks from differing traditions agree to a meeting, planning to appraise the cultural disparity in their practice and see what can be learned from one another. A small audience waits expectantly to hear what the men will say.

One, a Tibetan lama, sits very quietly on his cushion, fingering his wooden beads while murmuring, "*Om mani padme om.*" The second monk, of Korean descent, is well known for hurling rapid-fire questions at his students until they are forced to admit how little of the world they truly understand. At such moments he will often shout, "Yes! Yes! Keep that *don't know* mind!"

At one point during the meeting with the Tibetan, the Zen monk reaches inside his robes and pulls out an orange. "What is this?" he demands of the high lama. "Tell me, what is this?"

The Zen monk stands ready to dispute whatever answer the Tibetan offers. In his tradition, every preconception is instantly challenged, and open-mindedness is the swiftest path to enlightenment.

The Tibetan just sits, however, quietly fingering his beads.

"What is this?" the Zen master insists, holding the orange up to the Tibetan's nose, turning it over and over in his fingers. "Tell me, what is *this*?"

No answer.

"What is this, *in my hand*?"

The Tibetan finally leans over to the translator who is assisting in the encounter, and the two men whisper back and forth for several moments.

Eventually the translator addresses the room:

"Rinpoche asks, 'What is the matter with him? Don't they have oranges where he comes from?'"

☾

Appreciatory Verse

An orange is an orange.
We are what we are.

Some of us think *way* too hard.
Which often gets us nowhere.

Really.
A fruitless act.

☾

Initial Commentary

To penetrate this koan we must first grasp the essence of the orange.

What is an orange? Sunlight and water. Various minerals. A small sticker reading "Florida Sunshine." Perhaps a bit of harmless chemical some underpaid grocery clerk sprayed on the outer rind to make it shine under the lights.

To penetrate further, it is advantageous to stand for a moment inside the shoes of the Zen monk. What size are these shoes? Are they comfortable? Fashionable? Does the master need to change his socks?

Finally, we must ask why we care. Who are these monks to us? Are we likely to meet them? If we did, what would we say?

(

The Sutra of Substitute Fathers According to Sensei John Ono Lennon

> A lot of us are looking for fathers. Mine was physically not there. Most people's are not there mentally and physically, like always at the office or busy with other things. So all these leaders, parking meters, are all substitute fathers, whether they be religious or political. . . . Maharishi was a father figure, Elvis Presley might have been a father figure. I don't know. Robert Mitchum. Any male image is a father figure. There's nothing wrong with it until you give them the right to give you sort of a recipe for your life.[1]

(

Intermediate Commentary

At age nine, after the death of *his* father, young Leonard Cohen cut one of the man's tuxedo ties into small pieces. He then wrote a message on a piece of paper, sewed the message into a scrap

---

1. John Lennon, interview by David Sheff, *Playboy* 36, no. 1 (1980): 237.

from the tie, and buried it in his Montreal backyard. "I had a very Messianic childhood," the Canadian songwriter once explained. "I was told I was a descendant of Aaron, the high priest."

We don't know what Leonard Cohen wrote on that scrap of paper—his first song lyric perhaps—but the death of his father started Cohen on a lifelong search for meaning and structure, culminating, despite Cohen's biblical bloodline, in thirty years of study at the Mount Baldy Zen Center.

This story raises an interesting theological question. Isn't Mount Baldy a peculiar name for a Buddhist monastery? Can you think of other evidence that the divine force ruling our universe is particularly fond of irony? Or are we thinking way too much?

☾

Alternate Reading of the Koan

During the meeting with the Tibetan, the Zen monk reaches deep inside his robes and pulls out the hip bone of Leonard Cohen's deceased father. "What is this?" he demands of the high lama. "Tell me, what is this?"

The Tibetan just sits quietly, sipping deeply from a glass of water.

The master digs further into his robe, comes up with ex-Beatle John Lennon. Not the bones this time: the entire man. "What is *this*?" the Zen master insists, shaking Lennon right under the Tibetan's nose. "Tell me, then, do you recognize this fellow?"

No answer. Rinpoche takes another hearty gulp of his drink.

The Zen teacher, visibly exasperated, reaches behind the platform on which the two men are sitting and pulls out John F. Kennedy, Elvis Presley, and His Holiness the Dalai Lama.

"Who are these men? Tell me? You must know them. Which of these men is *your* father?"

Eventually the Tibetan leans over to the translator. They

whisper back and forth for several minutes, and then the translator addresses the room:

"Rinpoche has had too much water. He needs to pee."

❰

Concluding Verse

All these leaders.
Parking meters.

Full of water.
Each the same.

16

SON OF A BUSH

The dog pound of daddies, which is the political arena, gives us a President, then we put him on a platform and start punishing him and screaming at him because Daddy can't do miracles. **John Lennon**, qtd. in *Playboy* (1980)

1961

John F. Kennedy will always be the handsome father who died unexpectedly when we were all still young. We will forever wonder what might have been.

1963

Lyndon Baines Johnson stepped in to care for the family after our young daddy died. More of an uncle than a father; he was weird around the dogs and didn't look like us.

1969

Nixon, to be honest, was more like a stepfather. The relationship was awkward from the beginning. He never understood the kids.

1974

And after the divorce, what we needed more than anything was another sympathetic uncle. Enter Gerald Ford. Bumbling, yes, but kind.

1977

Then Jimmy. I suppose if you were from Georgia he could be your father, but for the rest of us he just talked funny.

1981

Ronald Reagan, finally, was a *real* father again. Loveable, winking, always ready to pull a quarter out from behind one of the children's ears.

Or maybe he was more the grandfather?
Didn't matter. He had that fatherly quality.
And it was pretty neat having a movie star in the family.

1989

George H. W. Bush always managed to seem like *someone's* father, but not necessarily ours. Maybe he was the dad who headed up the quiet Presbyterian family down the block—the clean-cut fellow who washed his car every Saturday morning, never cursed in public, and wore a sport coat and tie to dinner.

Seemed harmless enough.
But why was he married to Grandma?

1993

Bill Clinton was too young to be anyone's father (except Chelsea's), and anyway, the media making so much of the close ties Bill had to his mother left the indelible impression of a dutiful son. To us, then, he was the older brother. We were so proud of him. Such infinite potential.

But you know, in our family, it seems like we have a lot of screwups.

2001

Which brings us to George W. Bush. The poor man can't ever be a real father figure, because *his* father got there first.

It's tough working in the family business.

17

THREE DAYS IN SEPTEMBER

Monday, September 10, and President George W. Bush, already facing widespread criticism for time spent away from the White House (nearly two months out of his first seven, followed by a six-week vacation in Crawford, Texas) is fleeing Washington once again—this time to see brother Jeb, down in Florida.

I am loitering outside his house, by the front fence.

Humidity hangs heavy, like the interest on our national debt, and the sky is washed in a dull federal gray. The morning papers trumpet an economy in free fall and a rising unemployment rate. *Newsweek* is fresh on the stands with revived talk suggesting the illegitimacy of the president's hold on power.

"The sands of history will show Bush won by a single vote, cast in a 5-to-4 ruling of the U.S. Supreme Court," the magazine reports. "One justice had picked the president."

Worse, Justice David Souter offers the opinion that if he'd had "one more day," the vote might have gone otherwise.

Even the president's neighbors have been thorns in his side. As a gesture of friendship for Mexican president Vicente Fox, Bush capped off a lavish state dinner with a surprise fifteen-minute fireworks show. The unexpected explosions awakened and alarmed area residents, who subsequently complained to the police and the White House switchboard. The First Lady had to publicly apologize.

Maybe George W. kept fleeing Pennsylvania Avenue because very few people seemed to really want him there, or maybe he just didn't like the accommodations. He wouldn't be the first.

Warren G. Harding often insisted the White House was "a prison." Taft called it the "lonesomest place in the world."

The building does suffer a clear confusion of purpose. Part residence, part office space, part museum, the president's mansion must house a family, accommodate a remarkable array of business and ceremonial functions, and also act as a symbol of glistening history for some six thousand tourists each day. It is neither this nor that; neither here nor there.

For my part, standing at the fence that morning, I find it to be simply unimpressive. In the arena of national emblems, as a representation of our highest federal authority, domicile of the most powerful man in the world, the White House seems inadequate, disappointing, dwarfed by the grand architecture that surrounds it. The Washington Monument and the Lincoln Memorial are easily more majestic. The Old Executive Office Building next door is noticeably larger, far more ornate. The Capitol or Supreme Court buildings both serve as better, more imposing symbols of command and muscle.

The White House, from certain angles, resembles nothing more than an astonishingly luxurious high school—nicely landscaped, remarkably clean, but basically a squat building with thick pillars and a big front door.

Off and on, a light rain falls all along Pennsylvania Avenue. Tourists flock to the wrought iron fence, trading cameras to get "the shot," the prized photo showing them all smiling, standing tall, with the famous house framed just over their left shoulders.

Invariably the routine is the same. Tourists approach the fence, squint past the black rails for ten seconds or so, then scramble for the camera. The picture is the thing.

After the photo, some strain their eyes for a moment longer, as if they might see the president or his cheerful wife hanging around on the porch, but soon enough they realize this isn't going to happen. They move along, pushing strollers, consulting maps.

At one point, a man near me steps up onto one of the squat concrete barricades placed at the perimeter of the White House to deter truck bombs. He is just trying to get a better look.

A second later a deep voice comes out of nowhere: "Sir, get down from the barricade. Now."

I loiter near the fence longer than most people that morning, formulating my architectural opinions and contemplating George W.'s odd entrance into presidential office. Inevitably tourists begin handing me their cameras.

"Can you get a shot with all three of us?" some ask. Others, who probably can't speak English, simply point and smile, the intent clear enough.

I take about thirty tourist photos in my first hour, and when handing back the cameras I make use of the opportunity to ask people what they think.

"It looks small," a young woman from Israel tells me, a freckled college student in a Gap sweatshirt. "Not at all what I expected from the pictures I've seen."

Her friend, dark-skinned and possibly Arabic, laughs and shrugs. "They say the camera adds ten pounds," she suggests. "Maybe that's true of buildings too."

The bearded father of a large family group from West Virginia just shakes his head. "Not much to do here," he announces. "Big deal." I point him toward the Smithsonian Museum buildings up the road.

A few visitors are more positive. "Oh, of course, I like it very much," a man gushes in thickly-accented English. He and his five friends are from Kurdistan, he tells me. Kurdistan is not an official state, its people instead subsumed by Iraq, Iran, and Turkey. U.S. Forces protect some Kurds with our no-fly zone policy in northern Iraq, and this man is grateful to the president, the president's father, anyone in the big White House.

Across the way, in Lafayette Park, the benches are nearly empty, except for Frank, a retiree in a striped dress shirt and pastel blue shorts. Frank is feeding the squirrels.

"I don't know what it is that makes me like them so much," he muses, tossing peanuts here, there, and everywhere. "It must be the tails. I hate rats, you know. But the tail—now I like the squirrel's tail."

Frank is out here nearly every day, he explains with an extra-large grin, because "retirement is great." He likes squirrels, he likes tails, he likes Lafayette Park, and he likes being near the nation's most famous house. "You never know what might happen. Just last week a man tried to jump the fence."

Frank laughs and tosses another nut.

"I saw a picture of the poor guy in the paper. They had him tackled, all down on the ground and everything, within seconds."

Frank likes this sort of excitement.

What he doesn't like is the White House's window strategy.

"See that," he says, pointing to the north façade. "In one window the shades are open. In another they are closed. One window has the lights on, and the other has them off. They should be able to do better than that. You'd think they could get it organized so that all the windows look the same."

Perhaps the only person to spend more time across from the White House than Frank is Concepcion Picciotto. Picciotto—Connie to the handful of regular peace protestors who help care for her—has been sitting outside the presidential residence for more than twenty years, outlasting Reagan, George H. W. Bush, and William Jefferson Clinton.

Connie *lives* here, residing round-the-clock on a small patch of sidewalk in Lafayette Park, surrounded by yellow and green signs reading, "No more Hiroshimas," "Live by the Bomb/Die by the Bomb," and "No Blood for Oil." She is trying every possible means she can think of to get the president's attention.

A tiny woman, with dark, deep-set eyes and a prominent nose, Connie's face and neck are tanned and leathery from daily exposure to the sun. I have to squat down to speak with her, because she is huddled under a thick plastic tarp, sitting on a milk crate that serves as her only chair and upright bed.

"I must sleep sitting up," she explains to me, because the National Park Service has outlawed camping here. She averages three hours of sleep a night.

Another regulation states that someone must stay within three feet of hand-made signs at all times, or the Park Service can take them down, so only when friends come to briefly spell her can she ride her bike to the local fast food restaurant and use the free bathrooms.

I take a few more tourist pictures, and eventually, when one visitor suggests that "maybe it looks bigger around the back," I follow her to the rear of the building. But the White House doesn't look bigger here; in fact, the fence on this side keeps us even farther away.

The E Street side of the White House, closest to the Mall and the Washington Monument, serves as the primary entrance for those who work in the building and those arriving for official business. On either side of the fence are parking lots, guarded by armed officers and automated steel barricades. The barricades lower themselves to let vehicles pass only after guards check the identity of the driver, and then the car must stop just inside while a bomb-sniffing dog circles and looks inside the trunk.

The security measures are impressive, but they don't catch everyone. Tomorrow, September 11, 2001, will be six years to the day since a man named Frank Corder stole a single-engine plane from an airport north of Baltimore, headed south to Washington, came in low over the White House lawn, and crashed into a wall two stories below the presidential bedroom.

"For years I have thought a terrorist suicide pilot could readily divert his flight from an approach to Washington to blow up the White House," Richard Helms, former CIA director, worried at the time. "It has been said that the Secret Service is primed for just such a venture. Perhaps so, but the episode this week hardly gives one much confidence."

A few moments after I arrive at the back fence, a district police officer comes along and rapidly clears the sidewalk. "You'll have to move," he orders, his tone suggesting that we should move rather briskly. "You'll have to get across the street."

A young woman with two children has trouble complying with the orders—her youngest is refusing to get back into his stroller. I expect the officer to help her, but he is too intent on getting us out of the way. "You have to leave the sidewalk, ma'am," he insists. "You have to leave now."

She grabs her son by the elbow and yanks him along, panic filling her eyes.

Why we are being moved so abruptly is not at all clear, but once I manage to cross E Street, I see tourists pointing to the White House roof. Sharpshooters have appeared.

Inside the gates—though I only learn this later—the president is presenting Australian Prime Minister John Howard with a 250-pound ship's bell from the USS *Canberra*, a memento of the fifty-year military alliance between the United States and Australia. The ceremony ends, and the president shouts, "I'm going to Florida today" to the gathered reporters; apparently he is ready to leave.

The southeast gate is suddenly surrounded by motorcycle police, squad cars, Park Service jeeps, and police officers on foot. Everyone is on high alert. "He's coming out," someone says, so we head in that direction. The police spread their arms wide to show how close we can come and where we dare not go.

Moments later the motorcade starts to roll, including two long black limousines sporting American flags. In the second limo, through darkened windows, I catch a glimpse of the president himself, smiling a bit, waving to us from the back seat. He is slumped down, shorter than I expect, or maybe the seat itself is low in respect to the limousine window.

Whatever the reason, the president looks small, insubstantial; my first glimpse of him is as disappointing as my first glimpse of his postcard house.

(

The following morning I wake up in the Washington Wyndham Hotel, five blocks from the White House, and, as is my habit, I grab the remote by the bed to check the morning news. The president has landed safely in Florida and is planning to address some schoolchildren. Michael Jordan may be returning to the NBA.

I had gone to bed the previous evening confident that I knew exactly what I would one day write about the White House, secure that I had enough of a focus to write an interesting essay along these lines:

"The House seems small. The president seems small. The place has a way of shrinking a man."

An hour later I leave the Wyndham, locate my car, and drive a mile north to pick up my friend Ethelbert Miller. Miller, a prominent African-American poet, will be reading and talking to my students back in central Pennsylvania, and I am his chauffeur for the day.

We head north on Georgia Avenue about the time that two commercial airliners take off from Boston; we leave the District and enter rural Maryland around the moment the first of those planes slams into the World Trade Center in New York. A third plane hits the Pentagon as we pass Hagerstown.

We are just crossing over into Pennsylvania when the last plane is forced to the ground, perhaps by heroic passengers, only about fifty miles from where we are driving.

But we don't know any of this.

My car radio is switched off because Ethelbert and I are busy talking. We are both interested in politics, and conversation naturally turns to the performance of the new president. We give him mixed marks.

Both of us are worried about the situation in the Middle East, where Israeli defense forces and Palestinian police have been trading gunfire, and now missile fire, back and forth for weeks. Ethelbert experienced missile attacks in Baghdad some years previously, when he was there as a guest poet during the Iraq-Iran War. He tells me just how frightening an experience it was for him. "Americans are not used to bombs."

With the rapidly escalating tensions on the West Bank, Ethelbert is worried that terrorism will escalate worldwide.

"What you have to watch for is a change in the profile of the terrorists," he tells me. "If the faces of the terrorists change, that will tell you something. If the extent of the terrorism goes beyond where it is now, that will tell you something too."

Only later, when we stop for lunch in a small Greek restaurant, do we get a hint of how prescient Ethelbert's comments have been.

I begin to hear vague snippets of the newscast on a kitchen

radio: "heightened sense of security," "burning debris," "the president is in the air heading for an undisclosed location."

Eventually I ask the waitress "what the hell is going on," and she is shocked that we don't know. She has to repeat the news three times before we will even believe her.

Ethelbert's mother lives in the Tribeca section of Manhattan, a few blocks north of the World Trade Center. She is eighty-two years old, and Ethelbert is understandably concerned. He nervously punches her number into my cell phone.

"Mom, are you all right?"

She is well, it turns out, and amazingly calm.

An hour later, Ethelbert and I meet my students for class. We talk a little about poetry, a bit about the events of the day, but none of us can concentrate.

☾

On Wednesday Ethelbert needs a ride home, so we return to Washington, where sources are now reporting "real and credible evidence" that the third terrorist plane may have intended to hit the White House itself. Samuel Byck had tried to do just this during the Nixon years, but never got off the ground. Frank Corder succeeded in 1995, but in a plane too small to do much damage.

Perhaps the American Airlines 757 that slammed into the Pentagon had missed its actual objective—1600 Pennsylvania Avenue. The plane took a sharp turn just before the final moment, and maybe that turn was to find a secondary target.

The thought occurs to me that the relative smallness of the presidential residence may have saved the building. The White House is large, obviously, but not in comparison to the landmark structures on either side, and up and down the avenue. The White House might be difficult to pick out from the air, moving fast, coming down.

Unlike the dreary, rain-filled Monday of my first visit, the morning of September 12 is crisp, with temperatures in the sunny seventies and just a wisp of white cloud arching over Lafayette Park. The White House is surrounded by SWAT team members in black flak jackets, and the flags are all at half-staff. With the airports closed, no planes fly overhead.

The president is inside, holding emergency meetings with his national security team and members of his cabinet. The lonely house may have a way of shrinking a man, but today he is faced with larger responsibilities than anyone foresaw.

Slowly, as the morning develops, tourists begin to return in groups of three and four. They cautiously take the requisite pictures, but smiles are few and far between, replaced instead by tight looks of urgency and concern.

And slowly I see others arrive—not tourists, but local residents. While most of America remains at home, watching the awful footage played over and over on television, growing profoundly more depressed with each passing moment, a few Washingtonians are drawn outside, downtown, to the fence.

Perhaps they want to be witness to history.

Or maybe they just want to reassure themselves. The small house, the one with the thick pillars and the big front door—is it still there? Still standing?

18

WHAT YOU WANT, WHAT YOU GET, WHAT YOU NEED *A Post-Nixon, Post-panic, Post-modern, Post-mortem*

What makes the engine go?
Desire, desire, desire
Stanley Kunitz, "Touch Me"

Case Number

1341-PD-9

Deceased

Well, nobody is actually dead,[1] but things did not turn out for Dinty W. Moore in ways that he, or those close to him, expected.

---

1. Okay, that's wrong. Lots of people are dead, but you get the idea.

In fact things turned out pretty well. Concurrently, the planet did not explode, implode, or 'plode in any way.

This postmortem report will attempt to isolate some of the whys and wherefores of these unexpected results, or to at least make the discussion interesting enough that you stay on board through to the following chapter, which, in case you need enticement, will include Gene Simmons of the rock group KISS shouting insults at NPR's Terry Gross.

And an armed gunman.

Date of Death

The author's panic and intermittent paranoia began to die off near the end of 1984, but the process appears to be ongoing.

Cause of Death

Desire.

Location and Disposition

The deceased was found at home in his second-floor bedroom. He showed evidence of a recurring sinus infection, and his breathing was noticeably labored. Next to him in bed was his wife. The couple's teenaged daughter, Maria, was in the room next door. No drug paraphernalia was found in the home. No evidence of firearms. The deceased opened his eyes when medical personnel began to poke him in the ribcage, and he muttered something along the lines of, "unnh, ugh." Attempts to remove the deceased to the Blair County morgue were met with strong resistance.

Examination Type, Date, Time, Assistants, Attendees

Under the provisions of the Death Investigation Act, Dr. Hugh "Lumpy" Brannum performed a complete autopsy on Thursday, February 29, 2007, beginning at 12:05 a.m., with the assistance of Deputy Coroner Lauren "Kitten" Chapin. Also in attendance was Major Mahatma Gleet of the Hometown Police Bureau.

Special Circumstances

Due to the deceased's categorical refusal to proceed with the medical staff to the Blair County morgue, the autopsy was performed in the deceased's bedroom. It should be noted that the wife of the deceased was a considerable distraction, insisting repeatedly that Dr. Brannum and his staff vacate the home.

Presentation, Clothing, Personal Effects

Deceased was sprawled in bed, wearing blue plaid pajamas. He was badly in need of a haircut. On the bedside table, a water glass, half-full.

Features of Identification

There was some confusion at first as to whether the deceased was indeed who he said he was,[2] since his birth certificate listed a different given name than that used by the deceased in his daily life. To complicate matters further, Major Gleet of the Hometown Police Bureau remembered that a comic strip character once used a similar name. "Could be the same Dinty," Gleet cautioned. "I think when a cartoon dies we're supposed to call in Dick Tracy."

A heated disagreement ensued.

Findings

Mick Jagger was probably right.[3]

---

2. We'll stop calling him deceased soon.

3. You don't always get what you want, but if you try sometime, you just might find, you get something that works out just fine, even better than you thought.

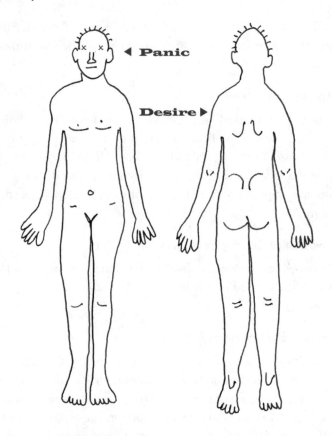

◄ **Panic**

Desire ►

Expanded Findings

In order to determine the precise cause of the unanticipated events previously enumerated, extensive external and internal examinations were undertaken according to standard forensic procedures.[4] The results are herewith broken down into typical anatomical units, more or less.

4. Dr. Brannum, a squeamish man with little actual interest in forensic science, would like to give special thanks to the authors of *The Complete Beginner's Guide to Human Vivisection* for many of the ideas expressed here. He would also like to express sincere gratitude to all members of the Hometown Police Bureau, especially Major Gleet and Captain Kangaroo.

Head

The United States and the Soviet Union did not, as widely feared, exterminate one another in a spontaneous thermonuclear conflagration.

Lungs

Our hero no longer smokes dope or, for that matter, anything else.

Upper Extremities

Ironically, the nation might have fared better had Richard Nixon stayed a bit longer in office.

Lower Extremities

Or maybe not.

Heart, Right Ventricle

The author remains married.

Heart, Left Ventricle

His search for an imaginary replacement father led nowhere.

Heart, Center

He is now a father himself.

Ears

George Orwell's *1984* failed to arrive in 1984 or 1985 or 2001, though some folks still see it coming just around the corner.

Eyes

Two. Malfunctioning.

Organ Weights

Seems like none of your business, really.

Hair

In fast retreat.

Further Expanded Findings

Head

The United States and the Soviet Union did not, as widely feared, blow one another to kingdom come.[5] Odd, really, given the paranoid rhetoric, legitimate dread, and taxpayer's expense devoted to the Cold War and the related nuclear arms race during the first thirty or so years of my herein documented life. (The author, it should be noted, is now writing in the first person, abandoning—for the moment—the voice of Dr. Hugh Brannum. The doctor is simply a literary device, different of course from the actual device Dr. Brannum used to crack open the author's ribcage during the home autopsy. Which did not happen.)[6]

The bad news, on the other hand, is that our nation's Cold War conviction that a major American city might be destroyed, at any unpredictable moment, by a superpower enemy has given way to War on Terror trepidation that a major American city might be destroyed, at any unpredictable moment, by some fanatic with a suitcase full of plutonium.

Lungs

Our hero no longer smokes dope, or anything else for that matter. He no longer snorts coke, swallows LSD atop tall buildings,

5. Though we came darn close. In October, 1962, when the United States discovered the Soviet Union positioning nuclear missiles in Cuba, President Kennedy sent a naval blockade and placed our military forces on DEFCON 2—the highest alert ever. Very scary stuff. Four days into the crisis, Fidel Castro cabled Nikita Khrushchev urging a first strike against the United States, in the event Cuba was invaded. The dreaded nuclear battle between two overarmed superpowers has never been closer to fruition than it was that week, but Nikita—a good guy after all—blinked first.

6. If you find these footnotes at all annoying, try reading them in a Swedish accent.

or looks for a hit of speed when he wants to stay up all night and play double-board *Risk* with a modified airlift rule.[7]

He's been dope free for years, yet oddly, or at least he thinks it odd, he still *dreams* about marijuana, maybe once or twice a month. Real dreams, of the sleeping kind.

Invariably the dreams go like this:

Dream Dinty walks into a kitchen, usually a yellow room, sparsely furnished, with a Formica-top table and linoleum floors. Brightly lit. On the table about a quarter pound of marijuana spills out of a clear, gallon-sized plastic bag, stems and seeds and buds. Dream Dinty smells it before he sees it. The sweet, leafy marijuana odor is overwhelming, and the moment it hits his nostrils he feels euphoric. Then he wakes up.

Smell is clearly a potent force.

Upper Extremities

As luck would have it, the nation might very well have avoided the multiple tragedies of September 11, 2001, had Richard M. Nixon and his band of merry plumbers resisted the temptation to break into various private offices. Nixon, a keen student of foreign affairs, had formed a panel to study future threats to the country, and that panel urged the development of plans "to protect the nation against terrorist acts ranging from radiological 'dirty bombs' to airline missile attacks." According to later declassified documents, Nixon's panel members "identified commercial jets as a particular vulnerability."[8]

---

7. In this version of the popular military strategy game, two Risk boards are lined up side by side. Kamchatka on one board connects directly to Alaska on the adjacent board. At the end of each turn, when a player has the option of moving armies from one contiguous country to another, he or she can instead opt to "airlift" armies to any country, on either board, in his or her possession. Trust me, it gets exciting.

8. "This is a real threat, not science fiction," National Security Council staffer Richard T. Kennedy wrote to Henry Kissinger in November 1972.

Of course Nixon and his government succumbed to various distractions in the second term—you know, impeachment hearings, Saturday Night Massacres, tape erasures, stuff like that—and nothing much was done with the recommendations.

Lower Extremities

Or maybe it *is* still better that he left.[9]

Heart, Right Ventricle

The author remains married.

A while back we bought a house. The house has wooden floors, top to bottom. One early summer afternoon, I walked in from work and my wife, Renita, was scrubbing those floors with Murphy Oil Soap—the same Murphy Soap my sister used to scrub the floors of that unpleasant apartment we moved into after my mother left my father.[10] I was sickened in 1965 and sickened once again when my nostrils sensed the same pungent smell numerous decades later. So sickened, the olfactory memory so potent, that I had to step back out onto the front porch and get my bearings.

But desire is potent as well.

9. "Tape recordings of conversations between Richard Nixon . . . and some of his top advisers during the first six months of 1972 have revealed him . . . musing about dropping a nuclear bomb on North Vietnam. In one segment . . . Nixon is heard discussing an extension of bombing raids . . . with Henry Kissinger, the national security adviser. Then, rather abruptly, he says: 'I'd rather use the nuclear bomb.' Whether Nixon was serious or trying to provoke Mr. Kissinger is not clear" (David Usborne, "Nixon wanted to drop nuclear bomb on Vietnam," *Independent [London]*, March 2, 2002).

10. See Chapter 4, or just take my word for it. In addition to soap, the J. T. Murphy Company produced a host of other oil-based products, including Murphy's Tire Mounting Lubricant. It is entirely possible, then, that at the moment my sister scrubbed the new apartment floors and I recoiled at the pungent odor, my father—working his mechanic's shift at Dailey's Chevrolet, entirely unaware that his life was being torn out from underneath him—was changing a tire using a J. T. Murphy product as well.

The woman in the window—the one who I imagined was already married (and thought, *Oh well*, then pedaled off), the one whom I eventually met by chance, then married myself, after proposing on the day my father was buried[11]—is extraordinarily tenacious. She wanted an honest relationship, despite all of my clever arguments to the contrary, and she wanted a real marriage, one where both partners pitched in and did the work. Imagine my dismay! She wanted to talk and share our deepest, darkest insecurities. Oh God! She wanted to stay married for reasons I have yet to fathom.

Stubbornly—her ancestors cracked boulders back in Italy, probably with their heads—she taught me how to fight, to argue, to shout, "Dammit, I'm not so sure I want to have children, so quit bringing it up all the time," along with other uncomfortable behaviors that keep marriages intact despite seeming unpleasant on the surface. She taught me the rewards of just sticking it out, enduring the lousy days, waiting for the good days that come along just in the nick of time.

And you know, they do.

If you wait long enough.

Heart, Left Ventricle

My ongoing hunt for a replacement father led nowhere, of course. The fact that I searched primarily on television, where people are not real and thus are entirely unavailable, had something to do with that. But I was born in the 1950s, raised in the '60s, and television was still a miracle back then.

Speaking of Murphy Oil Soap, by the way, here's another father figure I briefly favored: Mr. Clean, the bald guy on the bottle.

---

11. Any armchair Jungians who want to weigh in on the possible psychological subtext behind why a man might propose marriage on the day of his father's funeral can reach me by email: panic.desire@gmail.com. Really.

Mr. Clean was "stronger than dirt." He had biceps, fortitude, and dependability. He was always smiling; his bushy white eyebrows arched in pleasant surprise. It seemed that when I saw him on TV, he was clearly glad to see me too, in his cartoonish sort of way. And given my comic-strip heritage, why couldn't Mr. Clean be my dad?

My feeling—at age ten—was that it would have been better to wash the wooden floors in our new apartment with Mr. Clean, because Mr. Clean smelled fresh. Likewise, he would have been an entirely different father than the one I knew. He would have been steadfast, reliable. Everything at home would have been spotless and grand.

But as if to teach me a lesson—and life has this funny fixation on teaching me lessons—a few years back I became friends with the daughter of the man who invented Mr. Clean. This man—the advertising artist who first drew the jolly character to life—was Mr. Clean's human counterpart, or as close as I'll ever get. My friend Tracy revealed to me that Mr. Clean's creator moved away from his family when she was only five. All of his life he remained distant, hard to know. He wasn't much of a father. His marriage utterly failed.

Basically, the way I should have ended up.

So I was wrong about that, too.

Heart, Center

I am now a father myself.

That's one more thing the woman in that window[12] helped me to realize: you can't know if you'll repeat the mistakes made by your parents or not, so sometimes you just have to take a giant gulp of air and try something. Despite it all.

How is the father thing working out?

---

12. The one that I imagined was already married (and thought, *Oh well*, then pedaled off), the one that I eventually met by chance, then married myself, after proposing on the day my father was buried.

One night, not too long ago, Maria faced me in the hallway and barked, "I don't want to be here. I didn't choose this. I don't like it. I don't even like you. And I'm not just saying all this because I'm in a bad mood."

She's my kid; that's for sure.

It's working out pretty well.

Ears

George Orwell's *1984* failed to arrive in 1984 or 1985 or 2001, but as the George W. Bush presidential thrill ride begins to wind down and release its screaming passengers, plenty of good folks are still nursing a whopper of a paranoia hangover.

Remember the Patriot Act and the warrantless wiretaps?[13]

Remember the White House aide telling *New York Times* reporter Ron Suskind, "We're an empire now, and when we act we create our own reality"?

Orwell would have loved that.

Eyes

Television has to be given due consideration in any unconventional cultural memoir attempting to make sense of America over the past fifty years. A round-the-clock exposure to television (even when not watching, we talk endlessly about what we saw) distinguishes those of us in the Boom Generation from those that came before. Television is the glowing elephant in the room.

It was a big part of my life; certainly front and center for every culturally significant moment: Kennedy dies, the Beatles invade,

13. "There was of course no way of knowing whether you were being watched at any given moment. How often, or on what system, the Thought Police plugged in on any individual wire was guesswork. It was even conceivable that they watched everybody all the time. But at any rate they could plug in your wire whenever they wanted to. You had to live—did live, from habit that became instinct—in the assumption that every sound you made was overheard, and, except in darkness, every movement scrutinized" (George Orwell, *1984* [New York: Alfred A. Knopf, 1992], 6–7).

another Kennedy dies, Nixon is triumphant, Nixon resigns, Hinckley shoots Reagan, CNN declares war on Iraq, and oops, someone flew a plane into those twin towers.

The fascination of television, in my mind, is that television projects both ways—a bit like Orwell's telescreen, or a see-through mirror in a research lab. Television provides us with visions of who we think we are, what we value most, what concerns or fascinates us, on multiple channels, late into the night. But the reverse is true as well: we watch TV and inevitably want to become those glittering people. We want to wear the clothes they wear, style our hair as they style their hair, use the phrases our TV heroes make popular, and embrace the closely-scripted, never-a-dull-moment lives they seem to lead.

It's easy to see how this works with teenagers—how *Beverly Hills, 90210* or *Dawson's Creek* translates into high school trends and fashion—but how does it work when network correspondents peer from hotel windows to pinpoint bombs exploding in downtown Baghdad? How does it work when Fox breaks into regularly scheduled programming to tell us the vice president has shot his hunting partner in the face?

This stuff interests me.

Six months after 9/11, a Dutch gunman holed up in an office building, faxing out a statement explaining that he was demonstrating against widescreen television. The fax revealed that the man, presumed to be mentally ill, was angry that new TV screens were being promoted as "better looking than normal screens." Eventually, and sadly, he killed himself.[14]

But maybe he wasn't so nuts.

Consider the effects that television has had on our world, our culture, our children, our buying habits, our obesity levels,

14. Ironically, if you lived in Amsterdam, you could have watched all of this unfold on television. If you owned a widescreen television, the irony would probably have been more than you could handle.

our eyeballs over the past fifty years. Now magnify those effects, make them wider, brighter, sharper, more real.

Transform them into high definition.

Is that really such a good idea?

Organ Weights

Still none of your business.

Hair (The Musical)

Whatever we were marching for in the '60s—love, peace, free dope, "Nothing to kill or die for / And no religion too"—we utterly failed.

John is dead. There *is* something to kill and die for, it turns out, or at least far too many people think so. And religion still fuels the fire. At home and abroad.

"A brotherhood of man"? Don't make me laugh.

Imagine-ing did not make it so.

Maybe, then, we should have listened to Mick, instead of John: You can't always get what you want.

Which raises the real question: Did we get what we needed?

Summary Of Findings

The brain weighs 1,341 grams. Upon removal of the dura mater, the cerebrospinal fluid is clear. The superficial vessels are slightly congested. The convolutions of the brain are not flattened. No blood is found in the epidural, subdural, or subarachnoid spaces.[15] Examination of the cerebellum and brain stem shows no gross abnormality, or at least no more than to be expected after all that pot smoking.

Moreover, the world is a godawful mess.

Somewhere along my misguided way—I probably failed to recognize the turning point because I was stoned—desire crept

15. None of this has anything to do with the subject at hand, of course, but I wanted to prove that I knew the lingo (Dr. Brannum).

into my life and made me the little engine that could. I simply chugged along. Panic and paranoia crept out of my subarachnoid spaces and back onto the national stage. Where it belongs.

It's amazing how we human animals almost always find a way to keep chugging forward, generation after generation, despite all the good reasons to the contrary. The world seems forever on the verge of destroying itself, one way or another—pestilence, plague, world war, global warming—and we just put one clumsy foot in front of the other, marching, marching, bravely onward.

And so it goes, Mr. Vonnegut.

So it goes.

Official Cause of Death Statement

It is my determination that the more-or-less deceased party in question, Dinty W. Moore, had so little to live up to that he simply rose to the occasion.

Hugh Brannum, MD

19

"CURTIS KNOWS BEST"

Towering, Permanent, Perilous, and Soon to be Televised on a Widescreen Near You

SKYSCRAPER GUNMAN COMMITS SUICIDE

A mentally-ill gunman apparently unhappy with widescreen televisions has shot himself dead in an Amsterdam office building after a seven-hour siege. Early in the day the Dutch state broadcaster, NOS, said it had received a faxed statement from the gunman, who said he was "demonstrating against the manipulative sellers of widescreen television." A spokesman, quoting the fax, said he was angry that new television screens were being promoted as "better looking than normal screens." ***BBC News,*** March 11, 2002

In the March 2002 issue of *Harper's*, essayist Curtis White launches a long rant, chronicling his realization that neither side in the longstanding culture war really matters anymore. After years of battling back and forth like teams of rabid pit bulls tussling over a tatty rubber bone, the Ivy-educated pundits are superfluous. The future of American thought, White concludes, is now controlled by insidious forces smack in the center of the political debate.

While the rest of us were watching way too much television, White was busy dissecting the national intellectual discourse, and along the way he detected a treacherous band of "pragmatic, plainspoken, populist" villains, "moving, making its way, accumulating its forces, winning while putative conservatives and tenured radicals beat the bloody hell out of each other to no end at all." He calls this "third force" our "Middle Mind." "It is a vast mind," and he fears "it is already something towering and permanent on our national horizon."

You know, I read that in *Harper's*, and my panic and paranoia both momentarily resurfaced. The Middle Mind sounded entirely awful. I can't say for sure that I knew what White meant in the passage quoted above, but his words were inescapably menacing.

Towering.

And permanent.

Well, that's got to be bad.

Worse, apparently, this vast new evil is often indiscernible.

"It's not always easy to know when one is in the presence of the Middle Mind," White warns. "It generally flies below critique's radar because it has the advantage of not being associated with a particular political camp. . . . It has its effect without being noticed."

At this point the *Harper's* essay had me fairly white-knuckled, so to speak. White's essay was published in the shadow of 9/11, and the idea of something, anything, flying below the radar was bound to get our attention. Moreover, the idea that the evil was working beyond our notice brought up visions of some fresh form of chemical weapon, an anthrax aimed squarely at our intellect. Who were these pragmatic, plainspoken, populist scoundrels? I wanted to go out there and throttle them myself.

Until White came to his first name: Terry Gross.

"*Fresh Air* is not merely a promotional vehicle for the Middle Mind, it is itself a prime example of the Middle Mind in all its charm and banality," White complains in his essay. "Anyone who much listens to the show knows . . . that: 1) Terry rarely interviews an artist or intellectual that real-deal artists and intellectuals would recognize. 2) She has no capacity for even the grossest distinctions between artists and utter poseurs," and "3) The show is a pornographic farce."

Hold your horses, Curtis. Terry Gross may not be perfect in every way, but she presents a darn good radio show. Airing night after night, week after week, she probably *has* asked an insipid question or two, maybe hosted a few dubious guests, but in the end she interviews a wide array of interesting authors, seems to actually read their books (a modern-day miracle right there), and primarily talks about the ideas found in those books, not just the sales figures. I've always thought Gross was one of the good guys.

Then White threw out a few more names:

Humorist Joe Queenan for writing a silly book poking fun at baby boomers.

National Book Award nominee Louise Erdrich, author of *The Last Report on the Miracles at Little No Horse*, a work that White said "cozens its readers with the content of pulp romance."

pbs's *Antiques Roadshow* series—I thought White *didn't* watch tv—for having "turned arts and antiquities into crude commodity fetishism."

And Dinty W. Moore.

I had to read White's essay twice, and then call my wife into the living room for verification, before I could believe my double vision–suffering eyes. Like many writers, my day-to-day struggle is simply to be noticed, to have my words read, to believe that someone—*anyone*—cares about my next idea or bit of prose. To be listed as a menace, part of some insidious "winning" force in our culture, was alternately flattering, frightening, and unreal. If I'm winning, I thought to myself, I'd hate to know how the losers feel.

White, it turns out, was insulted by my book *The Accidental Buddhist* because I assumed my readers "wouldn't know anything about Buddhism," used a prose style that "works in novels written with Hollywood in mind," and failed to offer a sufficient amount of "intellectual content."

While I certainly wouldn't use White's exact words—I would have preferred *readable, vivid, common sense, run right out and buy one for your best friend*—what White accuses me of doing is pretty much exactly what I set out to do: compose a book for people who were curious but knew little of Buddhism, illustrating my various points with lively stories and anecdotes rather than philosophical abstractions.

I was befuddled. Flabbergasted.

I like those words by the way: *befuddled, flabbergasted.*

They make me laugh.

White probably wouldn't understand.

On the pages immediately following White's meditation on Middle Mind, *Harper's* reprints a partial transcript of a *Fresh Air* interview with musician Gene Simmons. Simmons, a founding member of the rock group KISS, is unambiguously rude to Gross during the interview, bragging about the number of his sexual conquests, insisting that Ms. Gross should put aside her books and get naked with a rock star in order to discover the true meaning of life.

This decision by the good editors at *Harper's* to run the Gross-Simmons interview just after White's Gross-bashing essay amused me almost as much as the fact that White had singled me out as one of the triumphant villains. I figured the proximity of these two items could be taken any number of interesting ways. Either (1) the editors agree that Gross is an evil Middle Mind desperado, and the fact that she let the insipid Simmons on her show in the first place just goes to prove it; (2) they felt guilty for letting White trash Gross, so they presented readers with a moment where she was clearly fighting hard against shallowness, one where she was a bit of a martyr; or (3) they were just having fun.

Whatever the case, White's rope of warning started to look like a slippery, slithering snake to me.

For starters, I didn't like the idea that White trashed Gross for not giving proper recognition to "real-deal artists and intellectuals." If he had a list of who was among the real-dealers, he should have shared it.

Joe McCarthy shared his.

I also wondered how lightweights, utter poseurs, and non-"real-deal" intellects lacking anything serious to say could be towering and permanent.

Are we exaggerating just a little bit here, Curtis?

Even though White took the time to pillory poor, defenseless authors—and I would like to publicly thank him, here and now, because the whole experience has been fun—I couldn't help but notice that his argument came back again and again to television. He criticizes me for my "Hollywood" prose. He attacks Gross for the fact that "many of the 'writers' she has interviewed recently have been writers for TV series and movies." If the Middle Mind had a motto, he supposes at one point in his essay, that motto would be, "Promise him culture but give him TV."

For my own part, I'd been watching more television in that part of my life than was probably advisable, partly because we were still in the dead of winter, partly because I couldn't shake a ghastly cold. I was steadily dosing myself with Robitussin, and all of those televised virtual images, combined with pseudoephedrine, were beginning to do odd things to my brain.

Which may or may not explain why I picked up my pencil and attempted to find a clearer understanding of this Middle Mind peril through the act of writing. I teach writing, mainly to very young college kids, and I constantly preach to my moping, apathetic students that writing is discovery, because I believe it. So I wrote.

What follows is the result.

I started with the BBC story on the poor gunman protesting widescreen televisions, and I imagined Curtis in the lead role. (White was obviously distressed, or he wouldn't have written his essay in the first place. Maybe he was *really, really* distressed.) I let Terry and Gene portray the hostages. I added a part for myself.

Though I admittedly took liberties in the editorial arrangement, the dialogue quoted below is one hundred percent accurate. White's dialogue comes directly from an interview he gave to Heather Freese, an intern at the magazine he edits (*Context*), and every line attributed to Gross or Simmons comes directly from the NPR interview, as reprinted in *Harper's*. My words are made up, but *I* made them up, so they are attributable to me. I quote myself accurately.

So strap on your Middle Mind, because here we go:

Curtis Knows Best

A Made-for-TV Docudrama

THE CHARACTERS

CURTIS WHITE: The thin, bespectacled skyscraper gunman.
GENE SIMMONS: A large man with long, kinky black hair. He wears clownish makeup, a leather codpiece, and he likes to stick out his snakelike tongue.

TERRY GROSS: A slender, bookish woman with short blonde hair and glasses. Highly inquisitive.

DINTY W. MOORE: A devastatingly handsome and fearless hostage negotiator. In his spare time he writes shallow books that appeal to the unwashed masses.

MAGGIE: You know her from the popular cartoon strip *Bringing Up Father*.

Act One

FADE-IN

Amsterdam—afternoon—establishing shot

INT. REMBRANDT TOWERS OFFICE

Curtis is holding a rifle in one hand and a television remote control in the other. He appears to be highly agitated. Hostages Gene and Terry are huddled in a corner, near the bookcase. Gene is crying; his black-and-white face makeup is tearstained. Terry reads a book—Louise Erdrich's *The Last Report on the Miracles at Little No Horse*.

CURTIS. This is so sad to me.

Hostage Negotiator Dinty enters, wearing a T-shirt that reads "I ♥ Middle Mind." Curtis, Gene, and Terry react with surprise.

DINTY. Okay everyone, please remain calm. We have a difficult situation here, but I think we can find our way out.

CURTIS. The only way that we are going to get out of this situation that we're in is to get smarter, to know more.

DINTY. Fine. If that's what it takes, that's what we'll do.

Hostages Terry and Gene are whispering in the corner of the room. Gene has his hand on his crotch.

TERRY. Let's get to the studded codpiece. Do you have a sense of humor about that?

GENE. No, it holds in my manhood, otherwise it would be too much for you to take. You'd have to put the book down and confront life. The notion is if you're going to welcome me with open arms you also have to welcome me with open legs.

TERRY. That's a really obnoxious thing to say.

Dinty, his face screwed up in confusion, looks from Terry to Gene. Curtis raises his rifle in a threatening manner.

DINTY. Listen, Curtis—may I call you Curtis?—you'll have to help me out here. I sense an extreme amount of anxiety in this room, but I can't tell what it is all about. Is the problem something having to do with sex? Is that what's going on?

CURTIS. The anxiety of the sex act itself leads to a general starving of the rest of life's erotic capacities. To me this includes architecture, landscape, an attention to pleasure, beauty, and creativity in every aspect. Look at the way we build buildings. They're just pieces of shit—purely functional.

DINTY. Okay, now I don't actually understand a lot of what you just said, Curtis, but do you mean that this . . . this . . . situation . . . is about the building we're in?

Dinty walks to a large, plate-glass window, angling sideways to study the exterior face of the Rembrandt Tower. In the background Curtis fingers the safety on his rifle.

DINTY. Curtis, you're right. It *is* an ugly building. But is violence the answer?

CURTIS. There is no best way.

Terry and Gene are still huddled on the floor, and Gene is running a finger through his tearstained face makeup, subsequently using the moistened finger to write "Gene loves Terry" on the wall behind him.

GENE (*to Terry*). I was going to suggest you get outside of the musty place where you can count the dust particles falling around you and get out into the world and see what everybody else is doing.

TERRY. Having sex with you?

GENE. Well, if you chose, but you'd have to stand in line.

TERRY. That's a really obnoxious thing to say.

Curtis walks towards Terry, crouches down beside her, and offers a comforting gesture. His rifle remains pointed toward Gene.

CURTIS (*over his shoulder, to Dinty*). For some reason, Americans seem to be terrified of sex.

DINTY. Well I'm not so sure that Terry is actually terrified. Perhaps she simply isn't attracted to Gene. I mean, he is ... peculiar looking. But Curtis, right now we need to focus on resolving this situation we find ourselves in. There are snipers outside—sharpshooters—and I don't want anyone to get hurt. I think you may be a reasonable man, so tell me ... about that fax you sent out a few hours ago. You said you were angry because the new widescreen televisions were being promoted as "better looking than normal screens." Is that the real issue here? You don't like big screens?

CURTIS. There's a strong correlation between television and depression, and we're not quite sure why that is. That's why I don't have a television anymore.

DINTY. So you're depressed? You know, we all feel a little low sometimes—

CURTIS. The problem is really suicide.

DINTY. Oh, that *is* serious. But we can find you some help. Why don't you put that gun down, and we'll walk out of here.

Curtis shakes his head no.

DINTY. Listen, have you ever tried Prozac?

CURTIS. My experience with antidepressants is that they work. I don't care why they work, they just work, and they have helped me in many periods of my life when I needed help.

DINTY. I happen to be on Zoloft myself. Fifty milligrams every morning, like a vitamin. Lots of people take antidepressants, Curtis. It's nothing to be ashamed of. (*Turning his attention toward the hostages in a clever negotiator ploy.*) Gene, are you taking anything?

GENE. Of course, don't I sound like a happy guy?

DINTY. Terry?

TERRY. Not really, to be honest with you.

CURTIS (*to Terry*). You can't really claim to be a serious or deep person unless you're taking Prozac.

DINTY. Now Curtis, that's highly judgmental of you. Perhaps Terry doesn't need Prozac because she isn't depressed. You said yourself that television causes depression. Well maybe Terry doesn't watch television—I mean she has to read all of those books for her radio show, where would she find the time? Hey, there's something you and Terry have in common—neither of you watches TV!

CURTIS. The stories are very much connected to each other.

DINTY. Exactly! Your story, Terry's story, even poor Gene's down there. We all have so much in common. We are a brotherhood of man. So maybe we can agree that no one is going to shoot anyone, right? I think we can forget our differences, whatever they are—architecture, use of pharmaceuticals, the relative size of our manly organs and television screens. Right, Gene? Right, Curtis?

Curtis sets his rifle down on the floor and embraces Terry. Gene begins bawling and sticking out his tongue.

CURTIS. Anti-intellectualism in this culture is as strong as it ever has been. In the same way, there's the fear of sex. So you can see how powerful the oppression is in this culture. It's so powerful that it has made us terrified not only of sex, but of the idea of eroticizing our life, of making our life beautiful, of making our lives creative, of making our lives important. Oppression is so powerful it makes us afraid of the potential of intelligence, and that's the only thing that can make us understand where we are and whether or not we want to be there.

DINTY. Curtis, I don't get a bit of that. Maybe I'm just too dumb. But I know you must be right, all those big words and everything. (*He walks slowly in Curtis's direction.*) Anti-intellectualism? Is that it? Is that why we are here? People are mean to you. They call you IQ-boy. Mr. Brainiac? That's why you sent the fax? Why you wrote that essay about Middle Mind? It's hard being the smartest guy in the room, isn't it?

CURTIS. If you're understanding it in a literary context, it's one thing. If you're understanding it in a pop-cultural context, it means something else.

DINTY (*still moving toward Curtis*). Great idea! We'll walk out of here, arm in arm, and sure the police downstairs will want to handcuff you, and eventually this will go to trial, but we'll get one of them O.J. lawyers, and we'll tell the judge that this was performance art, a pop culture paean to the excesses of network television, a brilliant reality TV spin-off called *csi: Amsterdam*, tonight's special guest is Gene Simmons, see him for the first time out of his makeup, and hell, if it is art, and by that I mean ART, well then it certainly can't be an intentional criminal act. How about that?

CURTIS. We are postmodern, like it or not.

Dinty snatches the rifle from where Curtis has left it on the floor. Gene and Terry react with relief. Maggie enters from outside the room, holding a rolling pin.

MAGGIE. Huh! It's that Dinty again!

CUE LAUGHTER

Play theme song from Father Knows Best

Actors join arms and run toward the studio audience, all smiles. The applause is deafening.

OPRAH. And guess what else? We're giving everyone a car!

The End

20

THE FINAL CHAPTER

As I was finishing the final chapters of this book, my father came to visit. The setting was a Chinese restaurant—one of those tacky American-Chinese joints decorated with pseudo-Asian murals, red tablecloths, and fat Buddha statues. My old man was seated at a large round table with three attractive women, dressed as if they were attending a 1960s garden-club tea party.

I almost never dream about my father, so this was indeed an event.

Dad, in a muted green suit, was dipping egg rolls into duck sauce, eating as if he had been denied food for most of the past twenty-five years. He looked a bit Nixonian, a dark growth of facial stubble on each cheek, his hair thick, black, and combed back from the forehead. He looked, in fact, like what you might expect if a digital artist morphed an image of a middle-aged Nixon with an image of my father as a younger man.

The three ladies had known me as a child—all of this was clear enough in the dream, though not discussed—and though they remained their crisp 1960s selves, as did my father, I was the grown fellow that I am today. The women seemed to know that I was a writer, that I had managed to publish here and there, and they seemed quite pleased for me.

"What are you working on now?" one of the women asked. Her name was Betty.

"A book about Richard Nixon and popular culture and misperception," I answered, "and about the many disappointments in my life."

Betty smiled. "Did you hear that, Bud?" she said to my father. "Nixon's dad never paid him much attention, and, come to think of it, you didn't notice Dinty much either."

My father shrugged, stabbed his fork into a platter of shrimp lo mein. Betty nodded and winked in my direction. The other two women reached for their cocktails.

This was a dream, and dreams have a warped sort of sense about them, but in this dream I was nothing less than overjoyed to see my father again. The feeling was palpable, more real than many of my waking emotions.

Dad seemed pleased to see me, too, and smiled a lot with his eyes, though most of his attention remained on the food spread across the table.

As the women chatted about one thing or another, I walked closer to where my dad was seated, fully expecting—since he had been dead for nearly two and a half decades, and we'd not set eyes on one another in all that time—that he might stand up, push back his chair, and give me a long-overdue bear hug.

Instead he grabbed for another egg roll, then turned his thickly-stubbled cheek in my direction.

I bent down, gave him a rough kiss.

Man, it felt good.

So here is what I think the dream was trying to tell me:

Don't eat chicken with black beans and garlic right before going to bed.

Or maybe this:

When you stop beating your head against the wall, your head miraculously feels better.

I had a father—not Mr. Green Jeans, not Mr. Nixon—but a real one, and much of what has been difficult in my life connects directly to his drinking and his absence. (If not, there's a string of therapists spread across the country who owe me refunds.) But if my demons and disappointments are attributable to Buddy, as everyone called him, then much of what's gone right must be attributable to him as well. You can't just give the man half credit.

I'll thank my Mom here, too. Nobody's perfect.

The point is this: These days I'm inclined to value the entirety, each piece of it. I'm starting to appreciate that my losses, let-downs, and wasted years were precisely what kicked me down the road like a bent tin can, until I ended right here, at this very spot, which is a good place to be if for no other reason than the fact that I made it.

So, life wasn't perfect. Listen, if you're lucky enough to be born rich, good-looking, and brilliant, what motivates you to get up each day?

I wouldn't know, but I find the question fairly amusing.

"So it goes," Kurt Vonnegut's narrator repeats throughout *Slaughterhouse-Five*, and for the moment I'm hard-pressed to come up with a better piece of wisdom.

This idea—value the crap in your life because that's what got you here, and if you're still here, well that's a good thing—works for the larger picture as well. Leaders die, presidents lie, nations clash, and terrorist madmen frighten us out of our wits. Hazy-crazy dreamers from the Summer of Love somehow morph into flabby baby boomers whose glasses are half-filled with either dentures or martinis. But the glasses *are* half-full. We've made it this far. Khrushchev could have taken us out in 1962, and wouldn't that have sucked?

Despite the disastrous cast of substitute fathers we've allowed into the White House, despite our abuse of aerosol and wanton disregard for Arctic wildlife, despite the evils inherent in wide-screen television, the world has not yet blown itself to smither-eens. History kicks us like a bent tin can down the road of panic and desire, and so we go, misperceiving wildly, onward to the next disaster.

And the one after that.

So, here's how that dream ends:

My father finally finishes his Chinese meal, wipes his grin-ning face with a red napkin, stands up, swaggers over, and says, "Dinty, my boy, you shouldn't have had to suffer all that gloom and confusion. Let me say right here that I'm sorry, it's all my fault, and I loved you more than anything. Still do."

Really?

No. The dream didn't end anything like that.

I kissed my father on his stubbly cheek; smelled the familiar aftershave, mixed with the scent of garlic and peanut oil; and must have rolled over in bed or something, because the dream stopped. Right there.

We were simply grateful to see one another.

It was the final chapter.

Until next time.

INDEX

forefathers, 9

journalism
    attraction to, 28
    fleeing from, 73, 87

Kitten, 10–11, 12, 13, 110

Leave It to Beaver, 4, 9, 10, 12, 13,
    38
Little Orphan Annie, 73–74

Manson, Charles, 4, 55–56, 58, 60,
    63, 65
Moore, Dinty W.
    as bad driver, 4, 47–49, 77
    in need of an alarm clock,
        28, 34
    swilling pseudoephedrine, 128
Murphy Oil Soap, 25, 117

nasty smelling stuff, 25, 40, 116
Nessen, Ron, 86
Nixon, Richard M.
    as assassin, 20, 39
    frightening the hell out of
        Henry Kissinger, 116
    never understanding the kids,
        96

Oprah, 77–78, 134
oranges, 90–91

Panic PA, xiii–xv

questions and activities, 33–34,
    73–74

Risk, 114

Saisho, Atsushi ("Ah so, U.S.A. is
    shit"), 67
Simmons, Gene
    discussing his codpiece, 130
    as imbecile, 126
    propositioning Terry Gross,
        131
suicide
    alleged, 21
    failed, 8–9

Thurmond, Strom, 56

upper extremities, 113, 115

Vonnegut, Kurt, 79, 122, 137

White, Curtis, 123–34

xenogenesis, 13–14, 34

Yorba Linda CA, 57

Zappa, Frank, 6, 14, 34

ABOUT THE AUTHOR

By now, really, you probably know enough.

In the American Lives series

Fault Line
by Laurie Alberts

Pieces from Life's Crazy Quilt
by Marvin V. Arnett

Songs from the Black Chair:
A Memoir of Mental Illness
by Charles Barber

Driving with Dvořák:
Essays on Memory and Identity
by Fleda Brown

Searching for Tamsen Donner
by Gabrielle Burton

American Lives:
A Reader
edited by Alicia Christensen
introduced by Tobias Wolff

Out of Joint: A Private &
Public Story of Arthritis
by Mary Felstiner

Falling Room
by Eli Hastings

Opa Nobody
by Sonya Huber

Hannah and the Mountain:
Notes toward a Wilderness
Fatherhood
by Jonathan Johnson

Local Wonders: Seasons in
the Bohemian Alps
by Ted Kooser

Bigger than Life:
A Murder, a Memoir
by Dinah Lenney

What Becomes You
by Aaron Raz Link and
Hilda Raz

Turning Bones
by Lee Martin

In Rooms of Memory: Essays
by Hilary Masters

Between Panic and Desire
by Dinty W. Moore

Thoughts from a
Queen-Sized Bed
by Mimi Schwartz

The Fortune Teller's Kiss
by Brenda Serotte

*Gang of One: Memoirs
of a Red Guard*
by Fan Shen

Just Breathe Normally
by Peggy Shumaker

Scraping By in the Big Eighties
by Natalia Rachel Singer

In the Shadow of Memory
by Floyd Skloot

*Secret Frequencies:
A New York Education*
by John Skoyles

Phantom Limb
by Janet Sternburg

*Yellowstone Autumn:
A Season of Discovery in a
Wondrous Land*
by W. D. Wetherell

To order or obtain more information on these or other University
of Nebraska Press titles, visit www.nebraskapress.unl.edu.